John Hanson Mitchell

THE WILDEST PLACE ON EARTH

Italian Gardens and the Invention of Wilderness

Drawings by James A. Mitchell

A Merloyd Lawrence Book

COUNTERPOINT

WASHINGTON, D.C.

Library of Congress Cataloging-in-Publication Data
Mitchell, John Hanson. The wildest place on earth ;
Italian gardens and the invention of wilderness / John Hanson Mitchell.
p. cm.
ISBN 1-58243-046-2 (hardcover)
ISBN 1-58243-215-5 (paperback)
1. Gardens, Italian—Philosophy. 2. Maze gardens.
3. Wilderness (Theology). 4. Mitchell, John Hanson. I. Title.
SB457-85 .M58 2001
712'.01—dc21   00-065947

FIRST PRINTING

Cover and text design by David Bullen

Printed in the United States of America on
acid-free paper that meets the American National
Standards Institute z39-48 Standard.

COUNTERPOINT
P.O. Box 65793
Washington, D.C. 20035-5793

A Merloyd Lawrence Book
Counterpoint is a member of the Perseus Books Group

1 3 5 7 9 10 8 6 4 2

THE
WILDEST
PLACE
ON
EARTH

for Jill, who endured

Contents

How wonderful it would be to live together in these
Rough fields, in a homely cottage, hunting the deer with our bows,
Herding a flock of goats with green mallow switches,
Here with me in the woodlands, you'd rival Pan for music.

Virgil, *Eclogue 2*

I shall never find in the wilds of Labrador any greater wildness
than in some recess of Concord . . .

Henry Thoreau

Prologue: The Labyrinth

It was easy to get lost in the mazes and labyrinths of the ancient world. Adventurers, explorers, hapless wanderers, and questing heroes entered the labyrinth seeking knowledge or adventure or even love, and some of them never got out. But the lucky ones who made it to the center and managed to find their way back to the world beyond the maze had often been provided with what was known in the language of mazes as a clew, which was essentially a ball of yarn or string. As you wove your way into the inner depths of the labyrinth you paid out the string behind you. After you reached the goal, as the center was called, you turned around and followed the line of yarn to find your way back out.

In some of the old folkloric accounts, the clew didn't work, or had unfortunate, unexpected results. Hansel and Gretel dropped a clew of bread crumbs as they wandered through the labyrinthine wilderness beyond their cottage, but sparrows ate the crumbs and they lost their way home. Eleanor of Aquitane used a clew to get in and out of the heart of the labyrinth where Henry II had hidden his mistress, the Fair Rosamund, with disastrous results for poor Rosamund. The first and best-known clew was the ball of golden thread given to Theseus by Ariadne, daughter of the ruthless King of Crete. Theseus worked his way into the center of the labyrinth, killed the Minotaur, and then found his way back out by following the thread.

The narrative line of this book follows, more or less, the same weaving pattern as a maze. That is to say, it begins at the beginning, at the entrance, and heads straight for the center, then makes a sharp turn and heads off in the wrong direction, only to turn again and begin back to the center on another route. In this

---

manner, it slowly winds its way toward its goal. The eleven courses, or paths, of the maze described in this book correspond to eleven chapters; some are long and circular, some are short, and almost straight, but eventually they all proceed to the goal.

It would be easy to get lost with all this wandering about, but I am providing herewith another version of the golden thread, a clew in words at the head of each course. Just walk on till you come to the end, and then read the clews in reverse order to retrace your steps and free yourself from the center—if you choose to leave, that is. Some may want to be lost forever. That was always the danger inherent in mazes.

THE
WILDEST
PLACE
ON
EARTH

I

Contact

CLEW: *Nature was here something savage and awful, though beautiful. . . . This was that Earth of which we have heard, made out of Chaos and Old Night. Here was no man's garden, but the unhandselled globe. It was not lawn, nor pasture, nor mead, nor woodland, nor lea, nor arable, nor waste-land. It was the fresh natural surface of the planet Earth.*

Henry Thoreau, *Ktaadn*

Years ago in the desert I met a wildman who claimed you could live forever in the wilderness with two or three milk goats and a working knowledge of wild edible plants. The idea of this, of taking off into the wild and living free and unfettered by the constraints and turmoil of the everyday world haunted me for a long time.

I had grown up in a town known for its gardens, a green, ordered world of old lawns, ancient copper beeches, and stone-lined garden pools with mysterious, unfathomable depths where golden-eyed frogs lurked. But it always seemed to me that there was some wilder place beyond the garden walls and that to get to the heart of things, really to know the spirit of nature, you had to leave this ordered world and follow the prophets of old into the wilderness, where a dry wind rattled in the tares. I thought the goat man was right. Now I'm not so sure.

A few years back, having had a few disheartening experiences in the American wilds, I began revisiting what our literary and artistic forefathers used to call the worn-out landscapes of the Old World. For a while I made an attempt to explore the national parks and wildlife sanctuaries of Europe, mainly in France and Spain. But in the end, I found that what I was attracted to most was in fact the most thoroughly transformed landscape of all, the hedged terraces, allées, pathways, pools, fountains, and hidden bowers of what was left of the old Renaissance gardens of Italy. And, ironically, it was here, among the clipped ilex and the canted, moss-grown stairways and statuary that I rediscovered that old sense of goatly wildness.

This return to the garden, I later learned, was the opposite of a parallel intellectual journey made by those who were responsible for the creation of our own wilderness preserves and national parks. In the mid nineteenth century, American painters and writers, who were originally taking their inspirations from pastoral Italian landscape and villa gardens, discovered—one might even say, invented—the American wilderness.

My understanding of all this began in a remote canyon in the American West. Having a bit of time on my hands, and a sense that I should get off to some wild place where there were no roads, I determined to walk a short stretch of wilderness in the Shell Canyon region of the Bighorn Mountains in Wyoming, a section of deep, echoing canyons, hard-running mountain streams, and dense growths of pines. I had in mind some version of the traditional sojourn in the wilderness, the grueling sort of hard travel that those seeking enlightenment or escape of one sort or another have practiced ever since we became human.

I packed all the necessary gear, gathered enough supplies to carry me through for a few days, arranged to be dropped off, strapped on my pack, and set out into the untrammeled wilds—free at last.

My thought was to walk on until I came to the end, a three-, four-, or maybe five-day sojourn. I would sleep in the high forest, listen to the coyote calls echoing in the canyons and ridges, make cowboy coffee in the mornings, and watch the sun hit the godless rock walls of the serrate mountains of the Bighorns. I planned to forge on day after day through this little-traveled part of the world, this deserted, high country, where I could be alone with the beating of my heart and have no one to talk to but wolves and bears and the little ground squirrels that would gather at my campsite each night. My intention was to get away from it all, to attain what is known among expedition leaders and guides as "the wilderness experience"—which, in so many words, means what Henry Thoreau called *Contact*—a sort of mystic sense of oneness with the deeper creative forces of the wild, the same thing the goat man told me he used to experience in his desert wanderings.

About three hours into this expedition I came upon a mountain stream. Actually, I heard the stream before I saw it, a dark, throaty growl that filled the trees and evolved into a deafening roar as I approached. The trail at this point skirted the stream and, at a narrow spot where it channeled through some sharp rocks, I found a crossing.

It was a good spot; ten yards downstream, the whole body of water simply disappeared over the edge of the world. There was sun in this place, it was still morning, the air was fresh, and even though I had hiked only a short distance, I walked over to the lip of the falls and sat down to admire the vista of green water, the great tangles of pick-up-stick logs that crisscrossed the stream below me, and the view out to the south, where I could see more mountains and cliffs, more peaks and valleys, and above them the big Western sky.

While I was sitting there, I thought I heard an eerie, ringing song sounding out above the roar of the falls below me. I turned and looked upstream and caught sight of a small dark bird, which promptly dove, headlong, into the rushing waters of the stream and emerged again. It was a dipper, a bird John Muir called the water ouzel, a sort of terrestrial, mountain-dwelling version of a coastal shorebird that lives along the wild streams of the West. I watched it work its way upstream, bobbing and dipping its body and periodically diving into the rushing stream—a small spark of life in the face of this great gash of boiling water.

I stayed in that spot for twenty minutes or so looking at things and thinking about the world I had left behind, and then made my way down the east side of the brook to have a look at the waterfall from below. In the rocks below the falls on the other side of the stream, I saw something large and brown and, leaping from rock to rock, crossed over to see what it was. There, wedged between some rocks, having fallen from above, was a dead bear cub.

The unlucky bear must have slipped while crossing the lip of the cascade and tumbled over. I meditated on this for a while, since I had been thinking of crossing the stream at that point too, and then I thought about the fact that this young, fat, otherwise healthy young bear had not made it into the world of adult bears. I began to consider what would happen if indeed it had been me who slipped, and I had not died in the fall but had broken a leg and lain there for days off the trail, which was more or less untraveled anyway, out of sound contact in any case because of the roar of the water, and how no one really knew where I was exactly in this isolated wilderness, and how search helicopters would weave across the sky looking for me and search parties with dogs would pass on the trail above but I would be unable to make myself heard, and how eventually, like this young bear, I would pass from this world with the sound of rushing water in my ears. Such things happen in the wilds. People go out for walks and die alone with the wind.

This reverie was not entirely healthy, I realized, and I began to wonder what, in fact, I was doing here in the middle of nowhere. This led to the whole question of purpose, and what are any of us doing here anyway, and why do we go back into the wilderness when it took us nearly a million years to get out of the wild and into civilization, and what are we, soulless biological creatures with no hope of enlightenment or human beings with a spirit and a destiny, and who are we, civilized, cooperative cultivators or hungry, self-centered predatory hunter apes?

Solitary treks into the wild bring on such thoughts.

One after another, these reveries led me onward as I sat there at the base of the falls, contemplating the awesome force of the cascade of green water, the immense overwhelming roar, and the death of the wild bear. By the time I got up to leave, I realized I had lost almost an hour of walking. There was no way I would make it to my planned next stop. But I carried on nonetheless.

About an hour down the trail I came to an open, south-facing ridge where I could look out over the landscape of the Bighorns. Here was the American cliché in all its glory—jagged, snow-covered peaks above a desert plain, the country of the Big Sky, a river in the middle distance, glinting with silver light. No people. No sign of any human intervention at all. With a little imagination I could see there on the flatlands a cattle drive trailing a plume of dust, or a single line of Blackfeet Indians moving to a new hunting camp.

I gazed out at this scenic vista and then turned around to look at a twisted pine clinging to the rock wall above me. There were little pinyon pine nuts all around me, some broken open and spread out on a flat shelf on the rock wall. I climbed up to look. The huge world of open America with all its hopes and dreams lay behind my back, but I found that I was, after all, more interested in the Japanese ink scroll of the twisted pine and the pattern of scattered seeds. Then I saw above me what appeared to be a cave, or rock shelter. Ah ha! I thought, an excellent lair for a mountain lion. So I climbed higher up the rock wall and, sure enough, there under the overhanging rocks was the scat of a large animal and a scraped area.

At the mouth of the cave I turned around and sat down for a while to look out over the landscape, and only then remembered the time. The sun was almost due south and I realized that at this pace I was not going to get anywhere. But then I didn't really want to continue. If I really wanted to experience this place, really appreciate it, it would take me a year to hike my intended route. After a little more cogitation on this matter and the whole question of purpose, and the meaning of discovery, I decided to change my plans.

What I really liked, I realized, was not that great rolling vista ahead of me, nor the country of the Big Sky, nor the rough life of a wilderness trekker in the tradition of the goat man. What I liked was adventure of a deeper sort, that longer, interminable exploration of the undiscovered country of the nearby. What I was hoping to find was not wilderness, or grand vistas, or a test of my own endurance, but a flash of that terrible spirit of place that often lurks in the most unlikely spots. I wanted a glimpse of the old gods of nature, the Great God Pan and his demon counterparts, and I was beginning to suspect that you can find Pan anywhere, even in the woodlots of suburbia.

In the end, I hiked back to the trailhead, picked up a ride to town, and went home.

I am not the first to come to this sort of realization, nor the first to turn around and give up on a wilderness expedition. In 1846, while he was still living in his cabin at Walden, Henry Thoreau ascended Mt. Katahdin in Maine. He started in the small Penobscot Indian village of Old Town, where, perhaps cynically, he asked the local Indians if they thought the spirit of the mountain, the entity they called Pomona, would allow him to climb the summit. From Old Town, he and his party ascended the Penobscot and Millinocket Rivers and then rowed across Quakish Lake and pushed on to the head of North Twin Lake, from which they intended to hike on to the base of the mountain.

They were in the true wilderness now. Katahdin had rarely been climbed by any white man, the local Indians avoided the heights because of the presence of Pomona, and no one in Thoreau's party had ever ventured into this section of the North Woods. But Henry was in ecstasy there. One night, under a full moon, rather than make camp they rowed the length of North Twin Lake, and rested on their oars, listening for the yowl of wolves and the booming of an owl. They then made camp at the north end of the lake, and Henry watched the ghoulish flicker of firelight on the woodswall as they prepared for sleep. They felt ill at ease here, as if they had reached the end of the world. That night a wind came up and blew the sparks from the fire onto their tent, and later that night, they were all awakened by an unearthly scream. One of their party had dreamt that the world was on fire.

The next day, alone, Henry began his ascent. He was on a quest at this point in his life. His brother had died two years before. He was living alone for the first time in his life, and he was now determined to become a writer. But more to the point, as he later explained in *Walden*, he wanted to cut life close to the bone, he wanted to experience the nature of experience. As he climbed upward, he thought of the image of Satan in Milton's "Paradise Lost," struggling up out of ancient chaos to the light.

As he got closer to the summit, clouds swirled in and engulfed him and then abruptly opened again to reveal the broken landscape of rocks and deep crevices. This was, without doubt, the wildest place he had ever been, a place beyond human and inhabited, he imagined, by gods. Here, Prometheus might have been bound for all eternity, while eagles tore at his liver. It was, Henry wrote, an unfinished place, not yet tamed for the human children of the gods. It struck him suddenly that he should not in fact be in such a place, a mere mortal in the abode of the immortals. On the heels of this thought, he heard a voice shouting out at him "Why came ye here, before your time?"

He had not yet reached the summit; it was still morning, but he made the excuse for himself that there was not time enough to carry on to the top and still make it back to camp before dark. And so Henry Thoreau, the bard of the forest, the man who gave the Western world some of the finest paeans to wilderness, turned around and went back.

Contact

Later on the lower slopes, he began to see the world in kinder terms. He envisioned the pastoral landscape of Concord, Massachusetts, the water meadows, the lily-strewn river, the fields, and his beloved woods. But he had been to the source.

"Contact," he wrote in his account of the event, "—rocks, trees, wind on our cheeks, the solid earth, the actual world. Contact, contact. Who are we? Where are we?"

These are ancient questions. Who are we indeed? Where do we stand in relation to the earth? And perhaps more importantly, in an urbanizing world, with wild places threatened around the globe, how indeed do you make contact?

The Great Forest

CLEW:

They stood in awe at the foot
Of the green mountain. Pleasure
Seemed to grow from fear for Gilgamesh.
As one comes upon a path in woods
Unvisited by men, one is drawn near
The lost and undiscovered in himself;
He was revitalized by danger. . .
Some called the forest "Hell" and others "Paradise";
What difference does it make? Said Gilgamesh.

      The Epic of Gilgamesh

After my failed sojourn in the wilderness of the Bighorns, I found that I was thinking often about this whole question of contact with the deeper currents of nature in relation to what the French Nabis painters used to call the banality of everyday life. Most of us are stuck in some indeterminate time between getting and spending with no space or time for reflection on the deeper nature of things, too crowded by daily routines, schedules, the noise of the media, the noise of traffic, the noise of music, or power tools, or trucks and planes. The traditional antidote to this was to find a place to get away from it all, someplace where you could think things through, and in both the ancient world and now again in the modern world that place was wilderness.

For those of us who live in a post-Walden world, the idea of wilderness as tonic, as release from these events, was summed up in a single, often misquoted, line by Henry Thoreau: "In wildness is the preservation of the world."

It is interesting that Thoreau did not say "in wilderness." There is, after all, as he perhaps knew, a difference between the two. The general argument, put forth most recently by the poet Gary Snyder, is that wilderness is an entity, a place, and a fragile place in fact, that can be very easily destroyed. Wildness, by contrast, is more deeply rooted. It is an ancient, life-sustaining current, a force of nature that can be most easily experienced in wilderness, but also lurks in the wilder corners of suburbia, or even in cities, and exists as potential even in some of the most barren, devastated environments. In wildness is not only the preservation of the world, but also the restoration of the world.

Wilderness, in any case, is an illusion; it is an invention of the garden. The whole idea of wilderness came along with the development of agriculture, some six thousand years ago. Although they may have held certain places apart, some special or sacred areas that they avoided or sanctified, the local Native American people who lived around my garden for some ten thousand years did not necessarily differentiate between that which was human and that which was wild; the two intermixed. It was the same for the nomadic tribes of hunter-gatherers who populated Europe and the Middle East during the Paleolithic and Neolithic periods.

By the time of the Sumerians in the third millennium B.C., after the development of agriculture in the Fertile Crescent, the concept of the forest or wilderness as a place apart was well enough established to become part of the first written epic, the story of Gilgamesh. In that account, the forest is evil, a place of wild, dangerous beasts, and it has to be cut down as a sign of the advancement of human culture over natural culture. The hero of the epic, Gilgamesh, goes into the forest, fights and kills Humbaba, the demonic forest guardian, and then, by way of victory celebration, cuts down all the trees.

But even as early as Sumeria, there was still something about wild land that had a draw, an attraction that entranced those living outside of the forest. Gilgamesh himself was bewildered by the place—in the original sense of the word—overwhelmed, confused, swept up in primal wildness. He and his friend, the wildman Enkidu, stood in awe of the greenery of the mountains when they first entered the wood where the forest monster Humbaba lived. In this uninhabited, savage place, Gilgamesh experienced the modern equivalent of self-discovery. He was, as one translation of the text reads, "revitalized by danger, and found the undiscovered in himself."

That is a fairly close description of the experience of the sublime as fostered by the nineteenth-century transcendentalists and taken up by the American painters of the Hudson River School and the painters of the American West such as Albert Bierstadt and Thomas Moran. It also describes exactly the current "wilderness experience" so sought after by harried executives and lost suburbanites of our time who sign on to wilderness excursions with outfitters who promise to take them to the uttermost ends of the earth where, in the language of one brochure, after trekking through the wilderness, the participants will "reconnect with the universe and the inner springs of personal light" (whatever that means).

By Biblical times, the idea of the desert, as in the Latin *deserta*, or wilderness, as a separate place was so well established that, even though it still had its old demons, it had developed a certain aura of power or capacity to bestow information or insight. The contrast to all this, the well-ordered and peaceful place where birds sang and fountains ran and all the trees bore fruit, was the garden, the traditional model for Eden.

It has been suggested by scholars that the image of Eden as it is described in Genesis was based on the realities of the Mesopotamian hunting park, an apparent peaceable kingdom where fruits could be plucked from the trees and lions and lambs lay down together. Eden was probably some known valley of the Tigris River in the vicinity of Babylon. It was a green strip of vegetation in an otherwise barren landscape made verdant by the use of irrigation canals that flooded the parks and extensive walled sections where the nobility and its retinue repaired to escape the hot summers in the cities. Within these elaborately controlled environments, the ruling gentry set up tents and even conducted the business of state—there were legal trials held here and religious observances and public festivals. The parks were stocked with free-ranging wild animals, somewhat akin to the open zoo system of our time. There were gazelles and lions and other local animals all living together in apparent harmony, since they were all fed artificially. The whole landscape, with its flowering trees, fruit groves, singing birds, well-watered gardens, meadows, and woodlands, grazing herds, and well-fed predators, was a stark contrast to the surrounding environment, the *deserta,* or wilderness. Here the uninhabited space outside the cities was deforested and overgrazed, a blighted, rocky landscape interspersed with dry hillsides, scattered flocks of sheep and goats, and a few dried-out water courses where the winds chattered and growled. In the *deserta*, nomadic pastoral peoples such as the Israelites tended their flocks.

But beyond the garden walls the old *deserta* maintained its lure. Elijah, John the Baptist, and Jesus himself, among others, went off into the wilderness to gain knowledge. Prophets came out of these wild places having achieved deeper understanding of the world—voices crying in the wilderness, prophesying wars or rumors of war. The garden offered earthly pleasure, sensuality, abundance, and ease. But wilderness offered enlightenment.

This idea of the wilderness experience, the now fashionable, often difficult, extreme (and, incidentally, expensive) expeditions with outfitters, may or may not (usually not, I've been told) provide the elemental "contact" of which Thoreau wrote. Similarly, private, individual expeditions into these regions allow you to throw off the noise of life, to touch the earth, to strip yourself of material goods, and to live close to the goat man and his tribe in an elemental, meaningful, essential existence. You may gain insight, you may make contact, perhaps. But in the end you have to come home. Although the memory may be there for a while, what have you really learned about living from day to day?

What is needed, I began to feel after I came back from the Bighorns, was something akin to daily contact, a life *in* nature, or a life *with* nature, rather than one of these extended wilderness sojourns, which require, ironically, and in fact perversely, the use of the highly advanced, energy-consumptive technology of flight to attain. The soothing effects of such expeditions may last at most a few weeks, and whatever lessons or insights were gained fade as soon as one gets back into the daily routine.

For a while I once lived in what might pass for wilderness, in a small stone cottage in the middle of a forty-thousand-acre tract of undisturbed, protected forest—the "Great Forest" as one visiting urbanite used to call it. The house was constructed of huge chestnut beams and gable ends of four-foot-thick native granite with little casement windows deep set in the stone. It was the classic woodcutter's cottage, something right out of the old fairy tales set in the Black Forest. The little dwelling was set at the end of a long dirt track off a forgotten hard-topped and potholed road that no one used.

For years the house had been inhabited by a state forester who lived there with his family, but eventually went crazy and had to be removed. I was told by the state authorities from whom I rented the place that the isolation was not good for his mental health. There was indeed something slightly eerie about the setting; it was dark, inside as well as out, with a huge walk-in fireplace, smoke-blackened beams, a heavy flag terrace outside the front door, and all of it surrounded by tall grim pines that moaned and whispered secret messages in the night wind. It would not be difficult, if you were already slightly off balance, to imagine that the trees were trying to tell you something, which, I believe, is what had happened to my predecessor.

The land around the cottage was all foothills and dark woods and hard-running streams that roared and howled during the freshets of late winter and early spring. These, coupled with the caterwauling of the barred owls, the periodic screams of something that I presumed to be a bobcat, and the unidentified crunch and crack of some heavy-footed thing that sounded out of the hollows below the house, merely added to the mystery of the place. I loved all this. My wife and I had just escaped from the forests of New York City, and I imagined myself a pioneer in the American wilderness. I would hunt bears here, and eat wild grouse, and learn to forage for mushrooms and spring greens. We would have a little garden where we'd grow potatoes, and haul water and chop wood and get back to the good life.

We did eat deer and grouse, bear and rabbits, but I never hunted them myself, and we never had a very good potato crop either, although I did learn to forage for greens and mushrooms. I used to set out every day in the morning, and then again at dusk, and range through the forest looking for food and adventure. I'd return at evening with a basket full of the roots of goldthread or sarsaparilla, and chanterelles and boletes, hen of the woods, sulfur shelfs, and the delicious, misnamed mushroom, the trumpet of death, as well as other forest delicacies.

My nearest neighbor was a forester who lived on the north slope of the hill, close enough for me to hear his dogs yelping at night, but not so close that I ever saw him, unless I wanted to. He lived with his family in an eighteenth-century farmhouse and supported his tribe with a meager state salary and by scavenging the forest. I actually learned a lot of woodlore from this man, some useful, some of it outrageous, as when he explained that there were many "vipers" living in a certain patch of land to the south. Charlie hunted deer for his meat (in and out of deer season, by the way), and when he had enough to feed his family he'd quit. He hunted rabbits and grouse, he trapped animals and sold their pelts, and he knew a thing or two about wild edible and medicinal plants, which he would bring home to his wife Elizabeth for preparation. Elizabeth favored sweets though; she used to make an unbearably sugary Norwegian pound cake that I ate only to be polite.

Their house was a bare, ill-furnished place. The large country kitchen where the family spent all their waking hours had a sagging, blanket-covered couch where dogs slept; there was a broken television in one corner of the kitchen that showed only a snowy pattern, but ran—seemingly—all day anyway, and there were many dogs, as well as a loose pet rabbit who lived inside the house to keep him from the foxes and bobcats. Elizabeth and her daughter Mary were always in the kitchen making something, joined sometimes by an apparent daughter-in-law who called herself Ansara. Periodically other collections of people from the surrounding hills would gather there, most of whom, I was given to understand, were family members. There were nursing babies, crawlers and toddlers on the floor, and outdoors you would come across wild, snotty-nosed, disheveled children in the weedy grounds between the house and the forest, and sometimes I would see a small, watery-eyed old man, unshaven and nodding on the couch among the sleeping dogs, somebody's uncle or father. Among all of these, the most frequent visitor was a son, also named Charlie, but known simply as C to the family.

Charlie the Younger had long, curly blond hair that cascaded around his shoulders; he looked very much like a self-portrait I had seen of the German painter and engraver Albrecht Dürer. His partner, or wife, was Ansara, a name shortened, I learned, from Ann Sara something. In contrast to Albrecht Dürer, Ansara was a Rubenesque figure, a heavier, more rounded version of Charlie the Younger, with curling, reddish hair, very wild, and seemingly uncombed for decades. They had an equally long-haired four-year-old son whom they had named Zeus, who ranged freely around the yard and surrounding forest like a wild animal. I once spotted Ansara and C cavorting naked by Hurricane Brook, having garlanded themselves with vines and sprigs of leaves. They were wrestling and splashing one another in one of the deeper pools of the brook and they looked for all the world like a satyr and nereid out of Arcadia, transported by some alchemy to the wilds of North America.

After the first season in that fairy tale cottage, in the style of the goat man, I grew interested in this question of the possibility of survival without reliance on the industrialized world—this was, after all, the late 1960s, and I was not alone in my thinking. The only difference is that, while many of my fellow back-to-the-land types were thinking about farming, I was considering the economics of hunting and gathering. All I ever did was think about it, though. I never hunted in spite of the fact that Charlie offered to teach me how to kill and skin wild animals and in fact encouraged me to "hang up a deer," as he phrased it. I would, however, eat those periodic windfalls that would appear in our little clearing in the forest. One evening just before dinnertime, a grouse came winging out of the greenwood and hit the kitchen window and died there. Charlie showed me how to pluck it and skin it, and we had it for dinner that evening. When he learned that I was fond of wild game, he and a friend of his who lived in the next valley began supplying me with food from time to time. I soon learned (again from books) the best recipes for squirrel stew and rabbit fricassee, and how best to cook bear and venison.

The first winter there was characterized by abnormally heavy snows. We were trapped periodically in our stone cottage for a week at a time, and had to hike to dig out the car, which we had left in a shelter near the road, since we could not get our road plowed. We had enough wood and plenty of rabbits and squirrels and rice, and it all seemed idyllic. I used to trudge into the woods on snowshoes and follow animal tracks for hours, and I imagined that if I had to—if I really had to—I could hunt these animals like Charlie or, even better, like an Indian. I could live well on nothing. It was, I suppose, that same mentality that drove the goat man to the wilderness. And it was the same sentiment that drew the first American pioneers deeper and deeper into the wilds.

The earliest, idealistic European settlers saw in this new world of the North American continent a fresh, clean, unspoiled landscape, a "virgin," as they phrased it, wilderness waiting to be civilized. George Perkins

---

Marsh, one of the first American conservation writers, pointed out that previous conquests of wilderness, as in Italy or Britain, had evolved over centuries, whereas here in North America a full-blown industrializing society with all its technological forces—steel axes and saws, picks and shovels and guns—burst in on an unspoiled land.

This American idea of conquering wilderness, of setting out for the territories, has now become part of the national character. The model of man (literally) in the wilderness is part of the American mythos, you see it in serious literature from *Moby Dick* and *The Adventures of Huckleberry Finn* to works by Ernest Hemingway, and you see it in the media, and you even see it in unlikely places such as cigarette ads, in the form of healthy, tanned cowboys riding horses in winter. Most significantly, I think, you see it in automobile ads in which everyday vehicles used by comfortable suburbanites to drive their children to school on paved roads are characterized by their ability to get through heavy snow and mud and to scramble over rocky dirt tracks in the deep wilderness. I daresay there were certain days when my wife and I could have used such a vehicle when we lived as we did in the Great Forest trapped by four feet of snow and with only a sad little Dodge Dart that we bought for fifty dollars to carry us to safety—and that parked half a mile away.

The myth of the wilderness endures, if only in advertising. More to the point, the myth has consumed itself. There are something like 400,000 miles of roads in the national forests of the United States, and the wilderness parks, where we supposedly go to discover ourselves and to restore our contact with the gods of nature, are now characterized by paved roads, heavy traffic, and rising crime, and are watched over by armed government guards with shiny boots, campaign hats, and two-way radios. Yellowstone, the queen of the American national parks, exceeds federal air pollution standards in winter because of the exhaust of the seventy-thousand-plus snowmobiles that cavort there each year.

The decline, or evidence of the decline, of wild lands was obvious as early as 1820 in America. It was clear even then to perspicacious individuals such as Edmond Ruffin, a contemporary of Thomas Jefferson. Ruffin looked at the eroded, gullied landscape of Virginia and foresaw a ruined continent in the future. But the first real voice of dissent, the first person to take a larger view of the abuses that American land was suffering at the hands of its newest immigrants, was Marsh, who documented his findings in a book called *Man and Nature* in 1865. Although there had been pamphlets decrying the silting of rivers and deforestation, no one before Marsh had put together so comprehensive an account of the total interdependency of human society and the natural world.

There is hardly a schoolchild in America who does *not* know of this now.

Nevertheless, the myth of wilderness dies hard. After he heard that there was a new cabin under construction about a mile from his house, Charlie Parsons announced, "It's getting awful crowded in this valley." I didn't tell him, since I still half believed in the myth myself, that the frontier closed over one hundred and fifty years ago, and there is no longer any way out, and that, in order to find the solace of open space, you have to look elsewhere.

3

The Garden in the Woods

CLEW: *The evident harmony of the arrangement between the house and surrounding landscape is what first strikes one in Italian landscape architecture—the design as a whole, including gardens, terraces, groves, and their necessary surroundings and embellishments, it being clear that no one of the component parts was ever considered independently . . . the garden was designed as another apartment, the terraces and groves still others, where one might walk about and find a place suitable to the hour of the day and feeling of the moment, and still be in that sacred portion of the globe dedicated to one's self.*

Charles Platt, *Italian Gardens*

The year after my Bighorn Mountains wilderness trek I learned of the existence of another sort of trail, a circuitous route that twists and turns so often that those who take it sometimes get lost and cannot find their way back home. For some travelers, time collapses on this ambiguous route, people become disoriented, and when, after who knows how many hours, days, or weeks of travel, they come to the end, there are even more mysteries. I've read old accounts of this journey that say that travelers have encountered a monstrous being at the end of the route, a man with a bull's head and a voracious appetite for human flesh. I've also read that those who walk this same path and reach the end have become enchanted by a sort of fairy queen who knows a charm that will bring snails out of their spiral shells. And one account I know holds that there is a door at the end of the trail and that door opens into another world, with even more bewildering, twisting paths. In other words, following this path could be dangerous; you may not return. But then all journeys have an element of danger. That is part of the adventure of travel.

Enigmatic, lost trails of this sort with their mythic demons and fairy queens are not necessarily located at the ends of the earth (although some would say they lead there). They can be found anywhere, even in some of the most civilized quarters of the Old World. I have such a trail in my own backyard. It is fixed on the southeast corner of a small plot of land, no more than thirty-five miles from a major eastern city. Rather than stretching off for ten thousand miles, it spirals ever inward to a center and takes the form of one of the earliest symbolic patterns in the human experience, the twisting course of a labyrinth or maze.

This particular labyrinth is at the heart of a garden I created a few years ago in a section of deserted land where no birds sang and nothing grew but white pine and toxic plants. Now the land around the maze is a sunny park where dragonflies skim the grasstops on summer afternoons and frogs stare at you from algae-covered pools and tall hedges border beds of scented herbs. Or so I imagine; the garden is not completed. But then what garden ever is?

My labyrinth, any labyrinth, is a symbolic representation of the route of the questing hero. It's an earthly map of the sun's way through the heavens, an image of creation in the form of the primordial snake with its tail in its mouth, a symbol of the life force, of death and regeneration. The maze path is a pilgrim's way, a route to salvation, to self-knowledge and liberation. If you follow the courses of a maze in a mindful way, and you walk on until you come to the end, you can gain insight, even enlightenment, which is essentially the same reason the prophets of old went off into the wilderness.

When I say garden here, I mean garden in the traditional sense of the word, that is to say a cultivated tract of country, as in, for example, the state of Lombardy, in what used to be called the pleasant garden of great Italy. I do not mean a yard, with a lawn and a flower bed here and a vegetable patch there and a clump of foundation plantings around the house. What I mean by garden is *place*, something you can get a sense of, a center, an intimate, organized space where you can go to get away from the world—not something that passersby on the road can see and then comment upon. My intention here, as it was in the traditional gardens of Italy, is to hold reality at bay, to create a metaphor, an invented world, and keep out those unpleasant things that pass by on the road and in the world at large.

Edith Wharton, in her classic *Italian Villas and Their Gardens*, which along with Charles Platt's earlier book *Italian Gardens* gave birth to the interest in Italian gardens in America, uses the term "garden-magic" again and again in her detailed accountings of the various gardens of the villas of the Italian peninsula. What she means by this is a sort of enchantment of place, an intoxication or spell that affects you in all the senses. She suggests that part of this effect may be the mere fact of time, of ancient history in an ancient land, but she says there is more to it, and that it is really a question of relationships, the way the garden is laid out in connection to the house, and the house and garden to the surrounding landscape, so that the whole becomes a composition. This was the great success of the Italian garden designs of the fifteenth and sixteenth centuries. Although they were refuges, often walled, and although they involved the use of geometric spaces, with hedges and topiary and artificial flumes and fountains, they worked with the existing landscape, they became part of a whole. And although to the modern eye they now seem abnormally controlled and orderly, to the Renaissance eye they were regarded as natural. Wilderness, or wild nature, was to the Renaissance mind a chaos that contained within it the essence of beauty, or possibility, which, with a little human assistance, could be fully realized. The Italian garden was an abstraction of the cosmos, an image of a more perfect world.

The land around my garden was originally a dark woods of white pine with a barren forest floor where the sun never shone and nothing grew but poison ivy. But some ten years ago on this two-acre plot of earth, using the design ideas of a nineteenth-century landscape architect named Andrew Jackson Downing, I cleared the dark forest—or at least part of it—and constructed a carpenter gothic "cottage" based on Downing's house plans, with four gabled wings, upper-story galleries, a porch, and a flag terrace. The cottage was tucked against the north side of the property and was meant to complement a preexisting garden that I had laid out on that piece of land over a period of years. The garden came first. Then I built the cottage to go along with it.

The origin of this garden concept came out of an early memory of mine, garnered from a book about heroic dogs, written, I believe, by Albert Payson Terhune, the creator of Lassie. My favorite story in the book involved an encounter between a pack of wolves and a domestic dog.

The adventure seems to have taken place at some outlying European estate with a grand manor house and French doors opening onto a wide stone terrace, cultivated gardens, and a surround of wild, deep woods. In the story, which was supposed to be true, a baby had been wheeled out to the gardens to sleep in the autumn sun, when suddenly, out of the dark interior of the woods, a pack of wolves emerged. The brave family dog charged out, teeth bared, and stood his ground in front of the perambulator, holding the circling wolves at bay until the master arrived and dispersed them.

What fascinated me about this was not so much the tale, but the setting; there was something about the place that fixed itself in my memory. I can still see in my mind's eye the old terrace, the raking autumn light, the colorful gardens (overgrown with wolfsbane, I now imagine), and, beyond the cultivated land, the deep forest where there was something wild and unknown and dangerous.

I realized that this simple image, inscribed in my mind through the written word so long ago, had somehow formed a model for an ideal house and garden and that, unconsciously, I had now recreated on my land a real-world version of this storied landscape—a garden in the woods.

All this is, as I say, still a work in progress. You come up the driveway to the cottage and you see an unkempt, weedy approach, all overgrown with wild grasses and asters and goldenrods, fleabanes and daisies. There's a wall on the north side rank with poison ivy and blackberry and winged euonymus—an ornamental plant that has gotten free around here and jumps into any uncared for garden corner. To the north and west of my cottage, which Downing describes as a "plain timbered cottage-villa" in his book *The Architecture of Country Houses*, there is a tangled wood. This north side was once a small hayfield with a deserted farmhouse in front of it. But over the years the farmer stopped cutting hay there, vandals burned the house one Halloween night, and now the tract has grown up to silky dogwood, aspen, and old arborvitae trees around the former house foundation. In the northwest, the woods are more natural, or at least older. There is a red maple swamp, dotted with vernal pools where wood frogs breed, and there is a dry woodland of oak and pine that ends in a dark hemlock grove.

As you approach the cottage from the road on the east, beyond a thicket of crab apples and plums, you can catch a glimpse of something in the back of the house, something enticing—a rose trellis, a bank of tall hedges, a patch of smooth green park with a surround of flowering trees and shrubs. What you see, mainly, from this angle is light, a green, wet light that contrasts with the dark surrounding woods, where, at least in summer, all light is absorbed. This is the main garden, and what I am seeking there is indeed light, a light in the forest. I want the forest too, of course, there would be no garden without it, and in some ways there would be no forest without the garden and you would not be able to see that wooded green wall where wolves might lurk. The Renaissance garden designers understood that interrelationship.

If you walk around to the back of the cottage—no simple thing since there are no grand entrances to the back garden—you will come to the enclosure. Here there is a high, square wall of trees—the natural forest, encompassing an open space. It's rough at the edges in some places, cultivated in others, and shaggy in the main—also by design, I don't want to get too formal. There are a few focal points, the main one being a summer house or tea house—also in the style of Downing. There is a rose arbor I scavenged from a project a few years ago; there is an architectural birdhouse, also in Mr. Downing's style, at one end; and then, just west of the main cottage, nestled against a wall of woods, is a small studio—which was actually the first structure on this property. Behind that is a little winding path that crosses over a wall and leads back into the woods. If you set out on this path, you'll come to another trail in the woods that circles around and eventually takes you back over a wall to the garden again. Here there is a tree-bordered path that leads to the tea house, which is enclosed by a little garden room, surrounded by flower beds. Through a break in the border, you'll come to a circular path, and if you follow that, keeping the tall hedge on your left, you'll come to an arch. That is the entrance to the hedge maze.

Long after I designed the garden in the back of this cottage I learned that what I had created out of my various and sundry preliminary designs actually had a name and was a style used in some Renaissance gardens—*pate d'oie*, or foot of the goose. The basic layout consists of an open, semicircular greensward just beyond the back porch and, radiating out from this open area, three allées, bordered with flower beds or tall hedges, with two squared garden "rooms" as they are called set off behind a wall of hornbeam trees.

This all sounds like a grand estate—which is the idea, of course, I'm trying to imagine myself a country squire who has retired to this spot to write his memoirs. But the fact is I did all the work myself and the whole project was accomplished with very little money and forged with hand tools bought at yard sales or salvaged from the town dump. Half the shrubs and perennials were castoffs or divided day lilies, irises, and peonies from the garden of a neighbor who is a plant collector. My "cottage-villa" was built partly from recycled material, and the garden ornaments and outbuildings were scavenged, stolen, or donated. It's all rough at the edges, and even though it's a new garden and a new house—or relatively new—it's aging well. It looks old. I want it to look old. In fact, what I really want here is a ruined garden, with fallen pillars, overgrown vines, and a mysterious past. The whole operation was theater for me, the cottage included, a grand, continuous masque, a fix in time, a way of stopping progress and holding the modern world at bay.

Half of the little suburban houses built around here in the seventies sought to have a place in the woods. Developers of that period did very little land-scaping, no lawns to speak of, with only a few crumbs of yew or rhodo-dendron scattered around the foundations. They actually cut as few trees as possible so that if you were to fly over the area, you would see only the trees and the black roofs of houses tucked in under the canopy. In fact in summer you wouldn't see much at all because of the tree canopy.

But recent fashions have been dictating the older ex-urban model in which you clear most of the native trees and plant wide expansive lawns and put up some vast edifice, some place that says—this is me, here, and I want you to know that I have made money in this life. I can't fault these house dwellers too much, since this is essentially the same attitude that gave the world the Italian villa in the seventeenth century. But the Italian villas were made to last, and had enticing, mysterious gardens. They were often designed, as at the Villa Lante near the town of Viterbo, with some aspect of the native vegetation left in its natural state, the *bosco* or *boschetta*, as it was called. This *bosco* served as a transitional area between the formal garden and the wilder landscape beyond the garden. Later in the seven-teenth century, English designers incorporated a similar concept, which they called, interestingly enough, the "wilderness."

In these Italian gardens, somewhere in the shrubbery or in the *bosco*, you could perhaps, on certain evenings when the air was thick, catch the faint, randy odor of goat, you might feel a vague sense of something about to happen, a presence nearby, and then suddenly you would glimpse, if only for a second, the fleeting image of Pan, the god of wild places, the Lord of the Wood. And later, in a niche hedged with ilex, you'd see him again, this time in the form of an old marble statue, his panpipes at his bearded lips and his little goatly horns protruding from a mass of marble curls.

You will not find Pan anywhere near the trophy houses of America. These structures are all internal, and the grand interiors are not so much the work of imaginative architects, but of electrical engineers—the *pièce de résistance* is not the garden, it's the media room and the high-tech kitchen. You must be among the elite to know this, you must be invited in, and, inasmuch as all the servants are electronic, you won't encounter any eccentric old gardeners here who will guide you to their latest plantings with pride, or sit you down by the wellhead and tell you stories of the werewolves or the witches that live in the hills beyond the villa garden. Nor can you leap over the garden wall to steal fruit from the orchard, or court the scullery maid here in America. You'd be zapped by some electronic surveillance device, and you wouldn't find any pears anyway, nor any scullery maids for that matter.

In the old days in Tuscany and the Roman Campagna you might at least have been chased out by an enraged, mattock-bearing gardener, or, as in some stories out of Boccaccio, you'd meet the old doddering lord of the manor himself and fall into a philosophical discussion with him, and he would give you fruit from his quince trees, and, while you're sitting there on the wellhead talking to the old fool, you'd catch sight of his beautiful daughter, and she would glance your way in return, and you would fall in love with one another, and you'd return night after night and scale the garden wall and meet by the fountain in the moonlight. Either that, or the lord would catch you in the orchard, challenge you, and then skewer you with his rapier. Maybe both.

The point is there's no imagination in the open, democratic yards of America. There's no possibility, no hope of danger, or encounter, or surprise. What you see from the road is what you get—mainly a smooth green lawn.

Although there were hedge mazes in some of the early Roman gardens, the idea of creating a labyrinth out of growing material became fashionable in the gardens of Europe in the late sixteenth century and reached its apogee in the Victorian period. But the actual pattern of the maze has far deeper roots. In its earliest form, the spiral maze, and its brother the labyrinth, appears on the walls of Paleolithic caves, symbolizing, it is believed, the life force, or the path of the sun through the heavens. The spiral form was associated with the goddess cults of the Neolithic and was closely related to natural forms—the spiraling horn of the goat, for example, and of course the snake. The form is universal; it was common in India, its image is described in the epic poem *Mahabharata*, and ancient maze patterns and labyrinths that were used to help women concentrate during childbirth are depicted in the *Chakra Vyuha*. The tradition endures to this day; I have seen white goats in rural areas of southern India with purple spiral mazes painted on their sides on certain festival days.

The form appeared later on temples at Malta, on tombs in Brittany, and in Ireland, and there was a great labyrinth constructed of mud walls at Lake Moeris, in Egypt, opposite Crocodilopilus, the city of crocodiles. Spiral mazes were cut into flat rocks and engraved on amulets throughout the Neolithic period, and by the time of the Romans, the Celtic religions were constructing stone and turf mazes in England and Europe. There are extant mazes in Ulmekaar in Sweden, and there is a famous maze, the Mizmaze, cut into St. Catherine's Hill in Winchester, England, that is part of a larger earthwork. There is some indication that the entire great mound of Glastonbury Tor was an elaborate, seven-ringed labyrinth. To ascend the hill you started up one circuit, followed another course, which brought you back down to the base, climbed once more, and so on, until this winding, circuitous path brought you finally to the summit.

All of these early mazes had spiritual overtones. The maze, either carved on rock or coins or laid out on the earth and cut into the turf, or stone, or hedging material, was related to the omphalos, the world navel, the primal snake with its tail in its mouth. In some instances these forms were used for oracular purposes. Some scholars—mainly the psychologist Otto Rank—believed this primitive symbolic image marked that transitional period in the course of human development when *Homo sapiens* began to emerge from animal nature to human nature. The maze was the beginning of art.

In recent years, new definitions for the words maze and labyrinth have emerged. It is held that the maze is a confusing, twisting path where you can get lost, and a labyrinth is a unicursal track where you can't possibly get lost. But traditionally, the two terms were interchangeable.

No matter how you look at it, the labyrinth form, along with the circle and the square, is one of the most elemental shapes, and although later in history they provided entertainments for the populace of many cultures, such as dancing places, mazes had their roots deep in the human experience and were not meant to be taken lightly.

It took me a while to decide exactly where to locate the hedge maze in my garden, but I finally decided that a section of poor ground in the southeast corner of the open backyard would be the best spot visually, even though the site is shady on the southeastern side. This meant that the entrance would face the back of the cottage, where there is a terrace and a porch. After much research I decided to base my design on a marble labyrinth in the Byzantine church of San Vitale at Ravenna, which was laid out around A.D. 530 when the church was built. The original is small, only about twelve feet across, and it is a part of the rich mosaic floor of the church. I enlarged this basic design and laid it out on paper, modifying it slightly to fit the land, and then, in early spring when the snow was off the ground, I went out with an armful of sticks and began staking out the courses.

I calculated that I would need at least one hundred and fifty plants to create this maze, and I spent a long time thinking about what materials to use. The finest hedge mazes of England and Europe were planted with boxwood or privet, and there is one in Ireland planted with yew. Boxwood is at the edge of its range where I live and is very slow growing and was beyond my budget anyway. Yew, of the type that grows in England, is not available here, and probably wouldn't live through the winter anyway, and privet, although hardy, was also a little expensive; if you laid this maze out straight, as a single wall it would stretch something like 250 feet. In the end, against the advice of my various plant advisors, of whom there are many in the region, I decided to use Siberian elm. It's a very hardy plant, able to withstand the bitterest winters, it's a fast grower, and if you keep it trimmed, it develops small, rounded, privetlike leaves. Most people, even a few experienced gardeners, don't recognize my trees as elms, since I keep them trimmed. This particular variety of elm leafs out early in the spring, and the leaves remain late in the season; I still have green leaves in the middle of November. Their biggest flaw, and the one that was readily pointed out to me, is that the trees break in ice storms. But since I intended to keep this hedge constantly trimmed, and since the trees would not be allowed to reach their full height of forty feet or so, I gathered that this would not be a problem. So after hunting through the catalogs, I put in an order with a midwestern wholesaler for two hundred trees.

They arrived, as all of these mail-order trees do, as little sticks with a few dried-out roots clinging to them. Had I not already had some experience with this sort of thing I would have said that they were either already dead, or moribund, and there was no hope that they would ever take. I heeled them in another part of the garden and began digging holes where I had placed the stakes—one hundred and fifty-three holes all told. Then, little by little, I began planting.

The stakes themselves had created an interesting pattern on the earth, especially when viewed from an upstairs window of the house. In fact, most of the modern mazes that are being constructed in our time consist of nothing more than stones, or stakes, or, in one case I know of, hay bales. But the little spindly, bare trees, with their little circles of fresh-turned earth around them, looked even better, and when—mirabilis dictum—in midspring the little sticks showed a flush of pearly green buds, they looked better still. By May they leafed out, tiny little mouse ears, all fresh and green and dewy in the mornings. I began walking there every day, looking them over, looking for trouble, but every single one lived.

Mine is what is known as an eleven-course, unicursal maze, which is to say it has only one, albeit convoluted, pathway with no dead ends, no tricks, or interior rooms, or false leads. Once you start, if you just stick to the path and keep moving forward and you don't turn around to see where you've been, or even where you're going, eventually you'll get to the goal.

Every year now, by April, the buds on the trees begin to break out. They're like little gray green pearls at first, or tiny green peas with a lined pattern where the leaves will be. Within a matter of weeks, they slowly begin to unfold. Some, I have noticed, are far more vigorous than others and these bud out first, and then all around the circuit the various individual trees follow suit. After a few years of walking these courses and tending these plants, I have come to know many of them individually, so that I could give them names, or address them in the personal pronoun—"*she* grows most fulsome" or "*he* has a lean and hungry look."

This leafing out offers a fresh flush of green, the traditional forest lacework of late April. It is an event that will not take place in the surrounding

natural woodland for another three weeks. But then this maze, and its surrounding garden, is my attempt to remake a world, to rush the course of
the native seasons with snowdrops and scilla, daffodils and tulips, and pro-
long the summer by planting things such as rue and viburnum and hollies
that hold their leaves longer or stay green all winter. This is a perverse
desire according to most of my nature-loving friends, totally unnatural,
unfashionable, destructive and the product of a humanistic, anthropocen-
tric mind, just like all of Western civilization. But I have come to enjoy my
perversity.

I had originally moved to this area about twenty-five years earlier and by
luck had found an old farmhouse set in the middle of an atavistic landscape
of working farms, which the tentacles of development had yet to encom-
pass. The place was, to put it mildly, a wreck. It had been built around
1810 from recycled wood and fresh-cut pines, and was so roughly constructed that the studs inside the plaster walls still had bark clinging to
them in 1997. The trees had hardly been trimmed of their branches, you
could still see the little stubs where they had been sawn off. The subfloor
had been built from planks that had been a part of some older dwelling
and then covered with wallpaper to seal the seams. That too you could see
after nearly two hundred years.

The land behind this house was surrounded by overgrown fields and
orchards and a deep tract of pine woods behind the orchards. The yard, or
what passed for a yard, was a weedy tangle of blackberry, wild grasses, and
a few old apple trees, underlain by thickets of poison ivy. A small soggy
pasture lay to the north, bounded by a stone wall, also rank with poison
ivy. There was a caved-in barn on the south side of the property, where

possums and raccoons took shelter, a fine grove of plum trees stood beyond the barn foundation, and to the west a mysterious forest of dark pines rolled up over the hill and down the other side.

I moved into this house during the month of August and the first morning after sleeping there, while the dew was still on the weeds, so to speak, I went out to look around. Immediately I came across some little sparkling bejeweled webs of orb weaver spiders. Barn swallows were sweeping to and fro across the yard, fallen apples were squishing underfoot, and the whole place seemed so wild, so untamed, and so ripe for adventure that I set out across the surrounding fields to look for more and see where it was I had settled. I did not then know that I had happened upon an undiscovered country and that for a period of time this was to be the extent of my world.

This particular property was located in a section of the town that used to be called Scratch Flat back in the nineteenth century. Partly because of a variety of accidents of economy, Scratch Flat held on longer in the face of development than most open spaces in the surrounding area. It was located in that edge between former wildland and farmland and the fast-moving suburbs. There were two dairy farms and three produce farms when I first came, and there were more farms east of the town, so many in fact that the numbered highway that cuts through Scratch Flat was designated as a scenic road—which is, of course, a relative term. This is not a country of scenic vistas and wild tumultuous mountains. You might not even notice the area except that it is now set off by the density of surrounding development to the south and north—small, high-tech industries that change so fast they can't keep their signs up to date so that they tend to announce the company that was there a month before rather than the current business. There are new houses on former farmlands and in woodlands where deer and weasels once ruled, and there is (or will be no doubt) more to come.

After ten years in my 1810 farmhouse, through the human version of cellular mitosis that seems to affect some nuclear families, my wife and I divided and re-formed, gaining in the process new husbands and wives, and additional children and dogs. Unlike many such divisions, however, since we both suffered some species of devotion to the place, rather than move away from one another we simply moved apart—a little. My ex-wife stayed in the old house and eventually restored it, maintaining the odd angles of the sagging door frames and old window glass and the crooked floors, and I simply moved into the traditional back forty. I constructed a little Thoreauvian-style studio for myself and lived there a few years before building the Downing-styled, carpenter gothic cottage-villa.

This amicable, slightly eccentric division became the subject of much dinnertime gossip in the surrounding towns, as did the collection of people who would gather in either of the two houses for Christmas and Thanksgiving, and sometimes again in summer. This collection involved former mothers-in-law, former husbands, ex-wives of former husbands, and doddering uncles from distant marriages, as well as, of course, the various and sundry children and dogs (dogs-in-law as one family member calls them) of the now recombined families. In the process, I believe, we were responsible for the creation of a new American family relative— the wife-in-law, or the husband-in-law. One poor visiting dignitary who joined one of our Christmas dinners finally gave up trying to follow this labyrinthine congregation, threw up his hands, and proceeded to drown his confusion in champagne after someone in our party was described as "my fourth wife's ex-husband's wife."

This assembly, this accretion, as opposed to separation, is perhaps unique in the too often squabbling, litigious, unhappy American society.

But among other cultures (and incidentally among certain bird species) it is not uncommon to experience what ethologists and anthropologists refer to as serial marriages. This seems to be particularly true among societies in parts of the world such as Tibet or western China, where arable land is at a premium and where the villages and cultivated plots are pressed up against mountain walls and surrounded by vast areas of inhospitable, untamable wilderness.

Not to stretch the metaphor, but in many ways, from the point of view of a land-based yeoman and nature lover such as myself, this was exactly the situation we were experiencing at that time on Scratch Flat, except that the wilderness in our case was urban sprawl, and the most dangerous predators were the land sharks and developers. We who lived there lived in constant fear of the bulldozer. We knew Scratch Flat was a doomed land, an anomaly. The place was on its way to becoming a suburban desert, with all its dangers, its rocky, unforgiving barrens of streets and parking lots, its water shortages, and its violent tribes of renegade brigands cruising their territory in high-speed vehicles throbbing with tribal chants from bass speakers.

Before I cleared the tract of white pines to put in the new gardens and the new house, I had seen very few species of higher mammals and birds on this property—gray squirrels, blue jays, and crows—and only a couple of plants—white pine, Canada mayflower, and poison ivy. With the new gardens came any number of new plants, some introduced by me, such as delphiniums and daylilies and peonies, and beds of herbs, and some uninvited but very much appreciated, such as the purslane and chickweed, dandelions, hawkweed, chicory, and Queen Anne's lace. Insects abounded on this newly cleared land: the exquisite little red-bellied dragonflies known as sympetron, green darner dragonflies, and ten spots, and snowy tree crickets, meadow crickets, and bush katydids, and all manner of flitting butterflies hovering over the flower beds on hot summer afternoons. The snakes came back—the garter and the red-bellied and the ringneck—and so did frogs, the green frogs and the bull frogs, wood frogs, pickerel frogs, and the little gray tree frogs that took shelter in the holes of the apple trees.

In the early years, in the old farmhouse where I had first lived, there had been a veritable grassroots jungle of small-scale wildlife. Now, in spite of my best efforts at neatness, it was all coming back again, the call of indigo buntings mixing with the rich scent of August mornings in the maze, the crickets chirping and the sparrows chattering, and the webs of the garden spiders, all dew-draped and bejeweled. It was a humane paradise, a garden in the woods, an Eden in spite of itself. And it was made all the better by reason of the surrounding forest.

Furthermore, as the farms of Scratch Flat were slowly abandoned, the wild forest and its accompanying seventeenth-century American denizens began to return to the region in full force. White-tailed deer, which as early as 1700 were scarce in the area because of cultivation and overhunting, were so common that they had become something of a problem. Wild turkeys, which had been extirpated from the region as early as 1690, now wandered through the garden plots in small family flocks each spring and autumn. Beaver had returned to the brook and marsh not far from this garden, and were so common as to create flooding problems for the newly arrived suburbanites who had settled in low-lying areas. And because of the beaver ponds and the abundance of standing dead trees, great blue herons began moving into the region and setting up rookeries. Some of these wild species were so numerous and so accustomed to human presence that they began to remind me of the animals that were associated with the traditional European and English estate grounds. The wild turkeys were like the peacocks of Italian gardens, and the white-tailed deer, who would sometimes graze in a small meadow below my cottage, were not unlike the roe deer of the deer parks of English estates. Even bears, which had been extirpated along with bobcats and mountain lions by the early nineteenth century, would occasionally wander through.

Along with these larger beasts, other common and not so common mammals and birds were returning to the area. The rarest of these was the fisher, a large tree-climbing weasel that had been driven from the region in the early eighteenth century and with the return of the forest began to appear in woodlots just beyond the suburban lawns. Porcupines, raccoons, woodchucks, and skunks returned, as well as a few animals that did not live here in the seventeenth and eighteenth centuries, such as opossums and coyotes. There were also new southern species of birds such as the cardinal, the tufted titmouse, the mockingbird, and the Carolina wren, along with resident birds such as great crested flycatchers and kingbirds.

This increase in forest-dwelling species was accompanied by a curious decrease in other species over the years that I lived there. When I first came, the air over the fields opposite the old farmhouse was filled with sweeping flocks of barn swallows, which had nested in an old unused barn in the field. The town cleanup crew forced the farmer to take down his barn because, as they claimed, it was a health hazard (what they meant was that it was an eyesore to the growing population of suburbanites). But with the barns gone, the swallows left, and as the fields grew up, with them went the bluebirds and the meadowlarks I used to hear in April, and also the little flocks of rising and settling bobolinks. Within a decade, things changed. Whereas we had once lived in the midst of old farms and fields, we found ourselves living in a forested ecosystem.

I knew that it was only right to have the woods come back. This is the natural order of things. Woods covered the land when the Native Americans held sway here, and in fact had existed for some ten thousand years, ever since the glaciers retreated. The English settled and cleared the forest, and by the 1840s the region was mostly fields. White-tailed deer became rare, coyotes or wolves were unheard of, and the moose and bears and fishers disappeared, as did the bobcats and mountain lions.

Yet in spite of this natural restoration, I found myself longing for the familiar rural countryside as the forest returned. After those first years on Scratch Flat I had come to realize that I actually loved a pastoral landscape far more than the gloomy woods where I had lived along with Charlie Parsons and company. It was dark in the Great Forest, we had to turn lights on in the cottage on rainy days, and it was darkest and rainiest in summer. I actually enjoyed all this for a while when I was there; I liked the traditional woodsman cottage with its atmosphere of the darkly Germanic fairy tales, liver-eating huntsmen, wild men with bear's heads, and the like. But the agricultural landscape of open pastures and farms of Scratch Flat was far more appealing. I loved the barn swallows that swept over the wide fields rolling down to the marshes of the brook below my gardens, and I loved the smell of fresh-cut hay that permeated the whole of Scratch Flat on afternoons in early summer. I loved the cluck of the hens I used to keep, the pastures dotted with cows, and the sheep that grazed on the western slopes of the farm on the other side of the hill. I loved that fading purple light that used to linger over the hills at evening, and the lion-brown fields of November backed by the dark walls of pines.

But how long could any of these natural ecosystems last? Every spring the insistent love song of the bulldozer was heard in the town—the high-pitched little warning beep of working machines. And every year, wood-lot by woodlot, field by field, the ten-thousand-year-old landscape of both woods and former fields was disappearing under an unnatural stone of asphalt as thoroughly obliterating as glacial ice. Then, finally, one sad spring, development reached Scratch Flat.

One day, walking on a tract of land not far from the brook, where I used to hear the booming of barred owls, I saw an orange ribbon tied to a branch. It was a surveyor's marker, the prelude to the fall of a forest. Immediately I snatched it away, as if to steal this one marker would halt the inevitable. Within the year, agricultural lands that had been farmed by one culture or another for some four or five thousand years on Scratch Flat were bulldozed flat and foundations were dug into the rich topsoil. All that summer the bulldozers marched to and fro across the landscape, like tanks across a battlefield. I could hear them from the sanctuary of my maze, pushing forward with a heinous roar, and then backing up with that horrid little warning beep that is emitted by backhoes, dump trucks, and other despoilers of the earth. It was a sad and unmusical farewell symphony that marked the end of one éra and the beginning of another.

A year after the first bulldozers appeared there were some twenty houses on the old farm. The next year twenty more filled up a forest section east of the fields.

And after that there were no more owls.

After years of fighting this seemingly inevitable march toward development, after joining with others to fight them lot by lot (and generally losing lot by lot), it occurred to me that the one enduring personal statement one could make in the face of this onslaught was to do exactly what I was already doing on my land, and that was to create a garden. So rather than embrace the traditional American solution and light out for the territories, I dug in. My idea was to transform my semiwild, American garden into a garden in the Italian style. It was an entirely perverse, objectionable, contrary, unnatural, and unfashionable experiment. Italian gardens were the rage in the 1920s in America, but no one that I knew of in the late twentieth century—when I began this project—least of all people with an appreciation for natural history, was planning this sort of garden. But then what I wanted to do was create more than a garden. I wanted to create a metaphor of order and balance to counteract the perceived disorder and imbalance that I saw in the world around me.

There was nothing new about this. The great villa gardens of Renaissance Italy were attempting to do the same thing. They were more than gardens. They were models of the perfect world.

4

In a Green Shade

CLEW:

What was he doing, the great god Pan,
Down in the reeds by the river?

Elizabeth Barrett Browning

. . . and then in that utter clearness of the imminent dawn, while Nature, flushed with fullness of incredible colour, seemed to hold her breath for the event, he looked into the very eyes of the Friend and Helper; saw the backward sweep of the curved horns, gleaming in the growing daylight, saw the stern, hooked nose between the kindly eyes that were looking down on them humorously, while the bearded mouth broke into a half smile at the corners; saw the rippling muscles on the arm that lay across the broad chest, the long supple hand still holding the pan-pipes only just fallen away from the parted lips; saw the splendid curves of the shaggy limbs disposed in majestic ease on the sward . . .

Kenneth Grahame, *Wind in the Willows*

I came to gardening rather late in life. My family had deep roots in the Eastern Shore of Maryland and was made up of two basic character types. One consisted of lawyers, doctors, and ministers who may have also owned farms, but rarely turned a clod of soil. The other was a race of sun-blasted yeomen who worked the earth from dawn to dusk for the duration of the growing season and were uncomfortable in the collared shirts and ties that they would don for funerals, weddings, and Sunday morning church services. I seem to have evolved from this latter stock, even though I grew up far from the Eastern Shore, in a genteel suburb where old lawyers and doctors puttered in their rose gardens on Saturday mornings.

But there was more to this evolution. We are all supposedly shaped by what psychologists call a critical image, a singular memory that can stand for the sum of your experience, usually in the context of a family situation. Mine takes place in a garden, in a green and leafy space, with the smell of boxwood, ancient ivy, and lime, and I am somewhere near an old potting shed, with a dry wood floor, dimmed light, stacked clay pots, mole traps, shovels, rakes, clumps of soil-caked beets, and braids of onions. Maybe I invented this place, maybe it's just an accumulation of images of various gardens I knew growing up, but at the core of this earthy environment, somewhere in that critical image, there is an éminence gris. He is an old Scotsman named Mr. Brunton, who worked as the sexton for the church where, for some twenty-five years, my father served as minister.

Mr. Brunton was not the classic kindly old gardener who patiently teaches the art of cultivation and in the process transfers the deeper lessons of life. Old man Brunton had little time for children and was hardly kindly; I can't remember that he ever smiled. I picture him now and I think of his cold blue eyes fixed under bushy white eyebrows, staring off, it seemed to me, into some middle distance. He was not even the official gardener for the church grounds, there was no such position as far as I know. But because he had a penchant for digging in earth, he had made himself into a sort of head gardener for an English estate rather than a sexton for a church, and through his efforts had caused the grounds of the church to blossom with flowering trees, clipped lawns, and groves of dark pines. He may have come to this country in a second wave of Scottish and English gardeners who were imported to work on the grand Hudson River estates of the late nineteenth century and who, it was said, had helped transform gardening traditions in the East.

Like any normal child I hated yard work (I hated all work for that matter), but from time to time, often as atonement for some sin, I was convicted to hard labor under the whip of Mr. Brunton, a situation that, I suspect, pleased him no more than it did me. He did not suffer fools or laziness lightly, and when I was with him he went about his work with the same steady pace, with virtually no attention to me and very little instruction; he simply expected me to tag along and do as I was told.

Mr. Brunton was one of those peasant types that you still can find in rural sections of the British Isles. He did not own work clothes, he simply dressed in retired suits and street shoes to work in the garden—light gray wool jackets, pin-striped pants, an ill-matching gray vest, and a white shirt buttoned at the neck, with the shirtsleeves rolled up. As the cooler weather approached, he would wear his suit coat, shirt and tie, and a soft cap cocked over one eye.

I never knew him as anything but old—a white-haired, gaunt figure with those piercing blue eyes and wild eyebrows, a hawk nose, high cheek bones, and skinny wrists and ankles. His one outstanding feature, the one thing that most remember him by, was a large, shiny bump on his forehead. This, I was told, was the result of a steel plate that had been placed inside his skull to patch a wound from a shell fragment that he had suffered at the battle of Gallipoli. The idea of having a steel plate in your head terrified me for years, and my two older brothers, learning of this fear, used it to torture me with an imaginative threat—"If you don't behave, they're going to have you taken to the hospital To Have a Steel Plate Put In Your Head."

We, of course, were not required to like this man; that was not part of the contract that my brothers and I were assigned. But I came to like him nonetheless, mainly, I think, because, unlike the other adults who worked around the church, he paid no attention to me except to reprimand me. His wife was a great rounded woman who adored the children who hung around the church, and would often give us chocolates. Sometimes she would grab me and pull me to her vast bosom and rock me back and forth while I struggled to get free. But Mr. Brunton kept to himself. In my mind, the closest image of him was the old grouch, Farmer MacGregor, the man who chased another one of my childhood heroes, Peter Rabbit, from the lettuce patch with a hoe.

Evenings in spring, when his church work was done, Mr. Brunton would go out and hoe his garden till dusk. He'd be out again in the early morning—I used to wake to the whir of his hand mower. He was always simply there. He was part of the architecture of the place, part of the land-scape, a moveable tree, a presence. He was still only on Sundays, when he would dress in black robes and stand by the bell tower door at the back of the church, staring forward toward the beflowered altar with his long-distance eyes, his white hair combed back for the occasion, and his steel plate bump gleaming in the half-lit environment of the church. I envied this part of his work. It was he who got to ascend the rickety stairs in the musty stonework of the tower and ring changes on the bells on Sunday mornings, a job I myself coveted, not so much for the bells, but because of the tower.

One of the great adventures with him, an event arranged periodically by my father, was to climb into this bell tower. We would ascend a sway-ing, circular wooden stair frame, between narrow stone walls, unfinished and dusty, with crumbling mortar, and pass through a hatch door onto the platform below the bells. They hung there above us like giant bats, silent, somehow ominous. The great adventure was to push onward, ascend a ladder on the north wall, with another hatch door above it, and then climb out onto the very parapets of the crenellated tower.

Sometimes we church rats would discover, to our joy, that old man Brunton had left the door to the bell tower unlocked, and at these times we would ascend without our guardian. From the parapet tower, we controlled the town. We were transformed in these ecstatic hours into medieval archers, drawing our longbows against the assembled invaders below us on the field of battle. We could see westward from this height to the streets and squared-off buildings of the business section, we could stare eastward to the hill where the larger houses of the community had been laid out, and it was, all of it, ours—we were the lords of this fiefdom. Until dinnertime, at least.

The town had come into its heyday in the 1870s, partly as a summer retreat for New York society. But with improved ferry service to the city, it gradually evolved into a wealthy suburb, and there soon followed a train of lesser lights from the Wall Street galaxy and some of the members of that rarefied culture of New York City society of which Edith Wharton wrote, and of which she herself was a part. For a short while, it even housed a turn-of-the-century socialist experiment organized by Upton Sinclair, an experiment that lasted no more than a year and that was charged with rumors of sexual license.

Just before the Great Depression, the financier Dwight Morrow, who was one of the partners of the J. P. Morgan firm, moved to the town and built an estate called Next Day Hill. He had just been appointed ambassador to Mexico and, most ethically, thought it improper to hold stocks, so he sold them all and bought bonds. Within months, the stock market crashed and he was suddenly not merely rich, but very rich. (There is a footnote here: Charles Lindbergh married Morrow's daughter, Anne, and the two of them retreated to Next Day Hill after their son was kidnapped. The media followed en masse, and at one point entrapped one of my older brothers and terrified him by grilling him on the whereabouts of the Lindbergh house, of which, of course, he knew nothing. He only knew to be careful of strangers.)

From our vantage point on the parapets you had a view of all the handiwork of the turn-of-the-century architects, including fashionable firms such as those of Stanford White and the landscape firm of Frederick Law Olmsted. Below the tower, close to the church, was my family's own humble dwelling, a square, gambrel-roofed building, with many interior hallways, passages, and hidden attics. Next door was a house in the style of Calvert Vaux or perhaps Downing. Beyond that, more high Victorian houses, and at the top of the hill, a vast great Greek Revival mansion with smaller, more recently built houses of lesser beings surrounding it, like the farm cottages of a feudal estate.

This territory was our battlefield and hunting grounds, a landscape of old gardens, huge trees, brick walls with secret gardens behind them, horse barns, and carriage houses, which, by my time, were old and deserted and accessible by means of broken windows and canted backdoors and cellars. The depression undid many of the families that had settled here. Some gave up and walked off the cliffs of the Palisades just after the crash. Some stayed on in decline, and some deserted their dwellings altogether and moved away so that, high above the town, in those grander estates overlooking the Hudson River, you could find the overgrown ruins of formal Italian gardens, collapsed pergolas, and old broken swimming pools filled with algae and frogs who eyed you from the detritus of sodden leaves and then ducked into the obscurity of the waters when you went to grab them.

We were the poor church mice of this world, fed and cared for by the remaining guilt-ridden stockholders. We used to fight over who got the top cream in the milk bottles, rich parishioners gave my father cars, and every autumn we were taken up the hill, quietly, to be outfitted with secondhand clothes by the widow of a rich man who had lost all his money and died suddenly.

In spite of our impecunity, I grew up across the street from a property landscaped by Frederick Law Olmsted and an environment shaped by the hand of Old World gardeners, with stretches of undisturbed woodland behind the carriage houses and along the Palisades above the Hudson River. For years I presumed that this town and our lives—with the boring round of school, and the children's Christmas concerts, and strange, long parties in cavernous houses in which normally sedate adults became loud and sang carols and spilled drinks on rugs—was normal. Now I see that the life we led in this fading glory was atypical. I grew up among doddering eccentrics, cat ladies living alone in grand mansions, a nation of mushroom collectors, watchers of birds (the Christmas bird count was initiated in this town), and gardens with crumbling ivy-strewn walls that smelled of must. The place held people in thrall long after they moved away.

This whole idea of taking a piece of wild earth and reshaping it to look like something else, the very thought of moving rocks, cutting down native trees, and replacing them with species that do not necessarily grow in that environment, churning up soil, and planting varieties of tropical and subtropical vegetables is in fact antithetical to sound environmental practices. But there seems to be something in the human soul that wants to make a garden. Even in prehistory there were sacred groves, sanctuaries, and arbors that were probably managed in some way to maintain them in their "natural" state, and these eventually evolved into more organized planted tracts, which in time became the gardens of antiquity.

Quite apart from the Garden of Eden and the famous hanging gardens in Babylon, which were watered by an elaborate system of irrigation from the Euphrates, there were many gardens in the past, some legendary, some actual, and they were all the product of a long evolution of plant experimentation and transplanting. There were papyrus and lotus gardens in the kingdom of Egypt, enclosed Greek villa gardens consisting of asphodels, lily gardens on Santorini, and fabled gardens at the very edge of the world in the kingdom of Hesperides, where golden apples grew on the islands of the blessed. In Islamic cultures, there were water gardens of tiled fountains and citrus. The Mogul empires maintained formal, private, watery sanctuaries, all green and flowery and shaded with ornamental trees that contrasted with the dry, stony hills of Rajasthan. Faced with similarly unforgiving environmental conditions, the Ottomans built walls and planted trees to protect and shade their beds of scented flowers, roses, and twining vines, all of which were laid out in patterned beds, an image that they eventually worked into the designs of their rugs and brought indoors. It was here, in one of these gardens, that Suleiman I first tamed the wild tulips of the scarps of Turkey, made it the flower of his court, fixed its image on his tiles and pots, and then sent its bulbs as gifts to the world beyond his courts. And even before all this, long before, there were the gardens of Shinto cults that integrated wild nature and tamed nature, and miraculous Chinese gardens featuring the lotus, the peony, and sway-ing bamboos.

During the same historical periods in which these gardens were planted—perhaps earlier in some instances—various cultures were setting aside tracts of land to protect wildlife, generally as hunting parks, although some of the earliest evidence of land protection or conservation seems to be associated with the preservation of sacred sites. Sacred groves wherein lurked powerful deities were respected even before the development of agriculture, and some of the oldest sanctuaries for wildlife in Asia were preserved from cultivation for religious reasons. There is still a vast deer park at Saranth near Benares on the River Ganges in northern India where it is believed the Buddha preached twenty-five hundred years ago. Hunting parks were common in ancient China, as in the Imperial Hunting Park near Beijing. The Père David's deer was probably saved from extinction because it was protected within this park.

The wild and the tamed, the sacred and the profane, all mixed in the garden, most especially, and most elaborately, in the metaphorical gardens of Renaissance Italy. And in no part of the garden, any garden, was this more evident than in a garden maze, where anything could happen — in theory.

The English word "maze" is probably of Scandinavian origin. There are similar words in both Swedish and Norwegian that mean to dream or to lounge, or move about in a unplanned, idle way. But in its oldest form the word harks back to wild land. It is related to a mental state of confusion, or "bewilderment," a word that has ancient roots in Aryan languages.

The earliest feudal villages of Europe were laid out in concentric rings, with the church, or, in earlier cultures such as the Etruscan, the temple, at the center. The placement of these centers was determined by the same geomancy that determined the center of a labyrinth, and some of the earliest Etruscan villages were in fact laid out roughly on the maze pattern. Outside these village centers were cultivated lands, with pastures just beyond them, and beyond the pastures, the forest. In the outlying sections of the forest lay what was called in Old French the *vild*. In northern Europe, this was an unpopulated section of as yet undisturbed forest with immense old trees, rock cliffs, sucking fens, wolves' dens, bears, and other dangers, some of them imaginary, such as dragons and waterbeasts in the style of Grendel, some of them real, such as escaped prisoners, mentally deranged outcasts, and brigands. During this time, Europe was still in transition from the older pagan religions in which priests and magicians venerated old trees and the myriad gods and goddesses of the forests and streams. Christian missionaries moving up from Rome understood this nature worship all too well and made a point of driving out the old way. In A.D. 725, for example, St. Boniface celebrated the conversion of the German tribes around Hesse by personally chopping down a sacred tree known as the Donar oak.

And what they could not destroy they assimilated. The old religion did not exactly die, it was simply transformed in the peasant mind into something dark and powerful. The forest became a place of evil, a Christian allegory for the world of sin and darkness, half pagan, and still associated with the old gods. In *The Divine Comedy,* Dante Alighieri passed through this dark forest at the very beginning of his journey through the three worlds of the afterlife, and even as late as the twentieth century, on Walpurgis Nacht, on windy, moonless nights, the Wild Hunt passed over the treetops—Satan and his hounds coursing above the deeper woods, baying and barking and pursuing the wild creatures and sweeping up into the maelstrom any unfortunate woodcutters or hunters who were caught out alone in the forest. One of the dangers of venturing out into these wild places, this *deserta*, this wilderness, was that you might return bewildered—which is to say rendered confused by wildness, lost to reason, overwhelmed.

The same thing is supposed to happen when you walk a maze. You are amazed, bewildered by all the twists and turns, you return to the ancient roots, the wilderness of that world beyond the village and its everyday life.

Shortly after I moved into my Downing-inspired, timbered villa, I began making a series of trips to Italy, mainly to visit my son who was living in Florence at the time, but also to accompany Jill, my affianced, an art historian who was researching images of the Annunciation.

Because of my family associations I was inadvertently immersed in the world of Renaissance art and found myself hanging around in the various museums and duomos looking at paintings of the Virgin and Child, while my bride-to-be studied the details of the wing patterning of the angel Gabriel as a part of her Annunciation research, and my son worked on a long-term project involving the symbolic statuary at the Boboli Gardens. On fine days, I would tag along with him while he crouched at odd angles to capture his decidedly untraditional portraits of the statues of Zeus, Neptune, Pegasus, and all the other gods, horses, and heroes of the classical period that are featured in the statuary of the Boboli. While he was at work, I would select a bench in the sun and sit there musing on time and the structure of the terraces and allées of this five-hundred-year-old garden. On one of these days, in a little forgotten nook of these extensive gardens, I happened upon a statue of Pan, with his pipes at his lips, his high, chiseled cheekbones, devilish eyes, and little goat horns. I had forgotten how much I liked him.

On rainy days, in the museums and churches I started looking for *mostri*, as they are called, the monsters that inhabit the darker side of Italian medieval and Renaissance painting. In a small cappella on the north side of the fine old church at San Miniatto I found a few blue devils torturing the damned. Several hideous beings were also torturing the damned in the Academia, and some poor devils were being stepped on by saints at Santa Maria Novella, while others were being driven out by the wrath of Christ. You see *mostri* and devils in the Uffizi Gallery in Florence, you see them in Sienna, they are in Rome, in the Sistine Chapel in Michelangelo's Harrowing of Hell scene; they're in Lucca, they're everywhere once you begin to notice them. Some have bat ears and whiplike tails with tufts on the end. Some are equipped with donkey ears, some have big teeth and pointy beards, with the ears of whippets and greyhounds. I found one high up in an obscure arch in Lucca that seemed to take the form of a blue elephant monster, and of course they appear in their various forms, all collected together—blue skin, horns, ears, trunks, hoof feet, claw feet, spiky teeth, pointy beards and all, in the myriad versions of the Harrowing of Hell—a favorite theme in Medieval and early Renaissance Christian art.

Among these, the king of them all, the Archdemon, always seems to take the same form, and as far as I could discern has had the same form throughout Christian history. He has horns and goat ears, a humanoid goatlike face with a pointy beard, and the shaggy limbs and hooves of a goat. I don't know why I didn't recognize him immediately when I first began to collect my *mostro* images. It was clearly my old friend and ally, Pan.

Of all the Greek and Roman gods, from Zeus to Athena, Apollo, and Artemis, Pan is the only one who would be instantly recognizable to the people of the twenty-first century. He is in fact the horned god that haunted the pre-Christian forests of northern Europe, the oldest and most powerful of them all, half man, half goat—the old Arcadian god of wild places metamorphosed by the magical alchemy of Christianity into the Archdemon, the Devil, and Pan's territory, the wild forest, transformed into the devil's domain. His image is still with us, either in his devil form, or with his pipes as Pan himself. It's an image we still recognize in Halloween costumes, on canned meat packages, and in the packaging of hot and spicy foods. Pan is everywhere.

My mother first taught me about Pan. She was a teacher of ancient history and a collector of Greek myths and legends, and I was introduced to this lively god at an early age. He seemed to be part of the family. My fondest memory of him came from a favorite volume my mother used to read to me, *Wind in the Willows*.

There is a scene in that story in which a baby otter somehow gets lost on the river and Ratty and Mole set out to find him. The two animals leave on their quest just after sundown when the riverbanks are alive with the chatter and rustle of small unseen animal populations. Their plan is to get to a weir upstream, a very dangerous place of rushing waters where they fear the otter might have gone. They row all night and with first light they hear a sound that brings Ratty up abruptly. It is a piping call, a bird song, a strange, new music. The dutiful Mole rows onward and soon they come to a point where the river divides, with a long backwater stretching off to one side. Rat hears the piping again, more loudly this time, and suddenly the Mole hears it too. He looks up and sees that Ratty is weeping with the beauty of the moment.

As they glide forward, the light increases, the meadow grasses shine, and the scent of the roses and the willow herbs and the meadowsweet fills the air, and then in the midst of this landscape they come to the weir, moor their boat, and push inland through the scented undergrowth until they break out into a little open area encircled by crab apples, wild cherry, and sloe. And there in the center of the clearing, in all his horrific splendor, they see "Him"—a towering form, his great curved horns sweeping backward and gleaming in the growing light of dawn. Asleep at the god's feet lies the round, podgy form of the baby otter. Then, as the sun rises behind their god, the two animals crouch down, bow their heads, and pay homage.

When they look up, he is gone.

This, I later learned, is one of the favorite passages in the literature of mysticism, and is often cited as a classic description of a breaking through the veil, a glimpse of the mystic netherworld. Significantly, the last thing that Pan does in that scene is bestow on the two animals the gift of forgetfulness. Ratty and Mole have no remembrance of Pan's role in the event.

Pan images are everywhere in Italy. He's in parks around the Villa Borghese in Rome and in villa gardens of the Janiculum. He's everywhere in museums. He's out in the Roman Campagna in the gardens at Tivoli. He's at Ostia Antigua. You see him at Herculaneum and Pompeii. He appears on the heights in the restored garden of Tiberius above Anacapri, and he's in the Boboli Gardens in Florence (and inside the Pitti Palace museum behind the garden as well). He's at Lucca in the little gardens, at Caserta in the big gardens, and almost anywhere you go in his various forms in Italy, and France, and anywhere the Romans established themselves, not to mention the Greeks, who invented him. He has even come to the New World. If you stand on the northeast corner of 71st Street and Park Avenue in New York City, with Central Park on your right, and look southward, you'll see him on the keystone on an arch. And if you walk on a block or so and go inside the Frick Museum, you see him again in his devil form tempting Jesus in one of Duccio's paintings. I've even seen him near home, in a pine grove behind the tea garden at the Fruitlands

Museum in Harvard, Massachusetts, not five miles from my own garden, a hideous, grinning statue of the ugly, old, lecherous goatman—my hero.

The real Pan was born in Arcadia in the remote valleys and highlands where shepherds tended their flocks. He was the son of the nymph Penelope (not the wife of Odysseus, a different Penelope). His father may have been no less a figure than Zeus, although Apollo figures in there in some myths, and Hermes is also a major contender, since he was very much at home in Arcadia. In fact there is a rumor that all of Penelope's various suitors managed to introduce some genetic material into this decidedly earthy god—the Greek word *pan* means "all." But it is more likely that his name is a contraction of the root word *pa-on,* which means herdsman and is the root of the English and Romance language word "pasture."

The lower half of Pan's body was goat—shaggy limbs and hooves—but he had the upper body and face of a man, except for a billy goat beard and horns. In other words, Pan embodied a Medieval devil image. Penelope fled in terror, it is said, when she first saw the baby she had produced. Pan is often confused with satyrs, who had a similar appearance, but the satyrs apparently began as humans and became animals, whereas Pan was mostly animal. He sounds a great deal like Gilgamesh's good friend Enkidu, who was a half-human, half-forest creature. The big difference is that Enkidu was seduced by a woman and became more human, whereas Pan was a great lecher who seems to have been unconcerned about who he mated with—nymphs, goddesses, shepherdesses, other goats, and even, via nightmares, nineteenth-century women.

Like his predecessor, Enkidu, he is associated with wild nature and inhabits that untamed zone of forest and rock just beyond the village boundary, where he cavorts with his fellow travelers, the satyrs and nymphs. Out there, in this legendary danger zone, the *vild,* or the unhoused wilderness that haunted the nightmares of European villagers for a thousand years, he is everywhere, and while you are in his domain, anything—a breaking branch, a sudden rush of wind, or here in the Americas the whirring break of a surprised grouse—will bring him to you in the form of *panic* (from the Greek work *panikos*, meaning "of Pan").

That's the thing about Pan. You don't always see him, or if you do, he will cause you to forget the incident, as he did with Ratty and Mole. Sometimes though, according to folklore, you can smell him, the randy odor of a horny goatman. And sometimes—often I think—you feel him. You go out to some wild place, some remote rocky hillside, a rushing falls, a deep glen, and you stand there in awe, and then something hits you, a sense that you are being watched, that you are not alone, and that something terrifying could happen here in this god-haunted site, this sacred patch of earth. That too is Pan.

I think I saw him once, years ago. I was taking a little walkabout in the Cévennes Mountains in the south of France and came across one of those ferny ravines with a fresh stream running through. It was hot, I had been walking for a while, and this fresh, bubbling stream, the shaded glen, and the mossy bank offered a cooling respite, so I took off my shoes, soaked my feet for a while, and then lay back on the bank. I fell into one of those dreamy half-sleeps there. I was dozing, but I still could hear clearly the riffles of the brook and, beyond the ravine, the high, incessant shushing sound of the cicadas, and far off, somewhere beyond the high walls, the distant clang of goatbells. Maybe I fell asleep and dreamed what came next, but suddenly there was a little cascade of rocks, I opened my eyes, and in the brush across the stream I saw a hideous, bearded goatlike face, with loose lips, great curling horns, and a human nose and mouth. I sat up abruptly and the thing, whatever it was, disappeared. I heard the clatter of loosed stones again, as if the beastman was scrambling up the ravine slope. And then the sounds of the brook returned; and the loud pulsing of the cicadas seemed to increase until it filled the whole hollow.

I presumed this was one of the many goats that range through this part of the world, but when I crossed the brook I saw no goat sign. In fact I couldn't find any indication that there had been any animal there at all.

The Cévennes region is rich in ruins. Everywhere I went I came across the remnants of one of the various cultures that had existed in this part of the world over the last two thousand years—nineteenth-century farmhouses, Medieval Christian churches, ruined monasteries, Roman walls and towers, even a prehistoric artifact or two. In the dry valleys and hills, there was still an aura of the classic pastoral, and there were many little herds of goats and sheep—you could almost always hear their bells on the distant slopes, and sometimes toward evening you could hear the sharp whistles and shouts of the goatherds bringing down the flocks for the evening milking. I could not shake the thought that I had seen something other than a goat, and that I had seen this face before somewhere.

Part of the beauty of wilderness, part of the attraction, is in fact this danger, the possibility of encountering the unknown. The nineteenth-century painters of wilderness knew that. They wanted to inspire what was known as terribilitá, a state of fear or ecstasy, in effect the sense of the sublime, an elevated emotion in the presence of power and beauty. The wilderness, especially in its first flush of discovery, in its purest state, can evoke this sensibility.

I have had intimations of wildness in my own backyard, thirty-five miles west of Boston in the form of coyote howls and owl chantings. I've seen the force of ancient waters charging up out of the earth in a spring, not two miles from my house. I've been terrified by night woods, heard the yowls and demon wails of unseen things in the woods behind my garden. And nightly in autumn, something terrible used to scream and caterwaul from the valleys below my stone cottage in the Great Forest. I've even found wildness in one of the oldest developed spots on earth, in the center of Florence.

One autumn day, I found myself at dusk in the enclosed courtyard of the little Brancacci Chapel of Santa Maria del Carmine, where the fresco of the expulsion from Paradise by the early Renaissance painter Masaccio is located. The subject of this painting matched perfectly the garden ideas that had begun to obsess me, the symbol of the garden where order ruled, as opposed to the wilderness into which Adam and Eve were cast after the Fall. This theme of expulsion from Paradise (which is related to the Persian word for garden, incidentally) has fascinated painters (not to mention Christian writers) from Massaccio and Giotto all the way to the American painters of the nineteenth century, such as Thomas Cole. It has even survived into this postmodern age in the works of the so-called environmental artists such as Robert Smithson and Allan Sonfist. To be thrown out of this garden and banished to the land east of Eden, where you had to struggle to encourage even a few fig or almond trees to grow among the dry stones, was to be cast into some form of living damnation.

Having viewed Masaccio's restored masterpiece, I retired to the little courtyard garden. The light was fading from the sky above the little enclosure, I could see dull streaks of gray against the blue, while below, here on earth, I was surrounded by a few clipped ilexes and a modest square of boxwood. I could not have been in a more civilized spot, a more controlled form of nature than in this place. Suddenly out of this gloom, the deep-throated bell of Santa Maria del Carmine began to toll a sad, slow vespers, and at the very moment, seemingly out of nowhere, black thrushes began to circle above the courtyard and then spiral down into the few clipped trees to roost for the night. They arrived in successive waves, black, fluttering forms slipping out of the pearl gray sky, singly and in pairs, until the whole courtyard was filled with chattering nightbirds.

Here, surrounded by the tragic tolling of the old bell and the swirl of black birds under a pearly sky and all this whistling and chirping and deep ringing, I suddenly felt the persistence of wildness, the survival of the natural world. The whole communion of life seemed contained in this mad swirl of birds. For a second, it seemed as if there were too many pouring in over these walls and that the world had turned to birds.

At that moment at least, the little courtyard seemed the wildest place on earth.

This equivalent of what the rough-hewn American outdoor guides like to call the wilderness experience, this sublime wild moment, is not supposed to occur in overly designed outdoor places such as the courtyard of the Brancacci Chapel, nor for that matter in any other garden. Except perhaps for the almost mathematical French garden, the Italian garden is, in essence, the exact opposite of wilderness. It is one of the most controlled natural systems on earth, with all its clipped hedges and its little gravel paths and its pools and fountains, pergolas, porticoes, and statuary.

The gardens of Italy evolved out of the Roman villa gardens, which were originally little more than an enclosed grassy park with a few trees, a wellhead or pond for irrigation, and perhaps a cool, pumice stone grotto. By the end of the Republic, however, Roman gardens had evolved into more elaborate, landscaped outdoor rooms, surrounded by the living quarters of the villas and interspersed with statuary, fishponds, and fountains, and a profusion of Mediterranean plants. These villas and their gar-

dens were scattered all across the landscape between Rome and Naples.
Most of them are gone now. Yet, in some ways, they live on: the ancient
Romans pioneered and perfected many of the garden ideas that are commonly used to this day—the concept of divided spaces, the use of ponds
and fountains, statues, and furniture, and, of course, plantings of a variety
of local and exotic plants. Some of these early Roman gardens were almost
wild in appearance, for example, the garden of Livia, the wife of the
Roman Emperor Augustus. We know a lot about the plants in this garden
since a fresco of it was painted on the walls of Livia's villa in Rome and has
been preserved in the Museo Massimo alle Terme.

Whoever painted the fresco possessed an intimate knowledge of plants.
Every tree, shrub, and wildflower is easily identifiable and can still be
found in local gardens, and in the wilds of the Roman Campagna. In the
foreground of Livia's garden there were daisies and hawkweeds and other
open-ground wildflowers—all in bloom regardless of the season, incidentally. Beyond this *prato,* as it is called, were plantings of oleander, myrtle,
boxwood, and laurel, and beyond this shrub wall, spruce trees, cypress,
pines, and oaks. There were also birds in her garden, partridges and
thrushes and European goldfinches. The original villa was located on the
old Via Flamina, and according to Pliny the Elder, it was the site of an
extraordinary event. Once while Livia was sitting in the garden, an eagle
flew overhead and dropped a snow-white hen with a laurel branch in its
beak onto her lap. Livia subsequently rooted the branch and the laurel
grew into the forest that supplied Rome with the laurel-wreath crowns
that were used to decorate the victorious generals, athletes, and emperors.

Some historians believe that the Roman love of gardens suggests that
the Roman countryside in Livia's time was already worn out and stripped
of its native forest. But there must have been remnants of the wild countryside at least in some sections outside the city. There was a little temple

to the Sibyl above a wild ravine by the waterfalls at Tivoli, for example, which is still standing in a remnant of wild wood. Tivoli is also the site of Hadrian's villa, which originally covered some 600 acres and was land-scaped with trees and flowers, grottoes, streams, canals, and pools, all of which were integrated with a complex of buildings. The place even now feels as though the gardens came first and the buildings were added later.

Unlike many of his predecessors, Hadrian actually made a point of vis-iting the provinces of his great empire, and spent much of his career trav-eling—sometimes on horseback, sometimes marching along with his company of soldiers. He went up to England, where he perceived the need for a great wall to keep the Scots out; he went down to Jerusalem, evicted the resident Jews, and founded a Roman colony; he traveled through Gaul, he went to Africa, and to Athens, and wherever he went he left behind public buildings, temples, and theaters. But finally he came home and built for himself a splendid villa outside Rome at Tivoli, where he spent the rest of his days laying out his gardens.

There is another notable restored Roman villa, on the heights of Anacapri at the northern end of the Isle of Capri. The villa once belonged to the emperor Tiberius and was lovingly brought back to life over a period of years by the popular turn-of-the-century Swedish doctor Axel Munthe, who ended up living there and eventually wrote a book about his life, *The Story of San Michele.*

The great gardens of the Italian Renaissance, such as the Villa Medici at Fiesole or the Villa d'Este at Tivoli, evolved out of these early Roman ideas and even began incorporating ancient classical statuary into the designs. After 1400, the Italian villa, which had its beginnings around Florence, came into its own as the watery, fountain-decorated, and uni-fied outdoor place that has been the model for the future gardens of the Western world. The Cortile del Belvedere in Rome, designed by Donato Bramante for Pope Julius in 1503, was one of the earliest of these "modern" Italian gardens and formed the basis for European gardens over the next two hundred years, until the advent of the looser, naturalistic formulas of the English gardens.

All of these classical Italian designs were based on the unifying concept of outdoor garden "rooms," which were aligned with the main dwelling and were intersected with other rooms, opening along axes and cross axes, and the whole of it strung together with terraces, paths, and flights of steps. There was no dearth of flowering plants in the original gardens of the Italian peninsula, but until recently it was believed that over the centuries these flowering gardens gave way to cool stonework and labyrinthine designs of ilex hedges, laurel, cypress, and boxwood, with arbors and pergolas, allées, and grottoes. Italy is not an environment washed with cool summer rains that permits the development of lawns and beds of flowers, and although there is some debate over the matter among garden historians, in time, it is believed, the gardens of Italy became not so much horticultural entities as outdoor dwelling-places filled with different little spaces where you could hide or sit in the sun for an hour—or in the shade in summer. Nowadays many of them have a certain down-at-the-heels quality. They may seem formalized and orderly, but even in the time of Edith Wharton they were in decline, with cracked walls, overgrown vines, and a romantic sense of place, a sense unlike any other garden in the world. As Wharton suggested, if you can find yourself alone in one of them, you may get the feeling that something might have happened in this spot, a seduction, a duel, a poisoning, a Machiavellian plot. Trysts abounded in these places, as in the stories of Boccaccio, or Hawthorne's dark tale "The Secret Garden," in which the hero falls in love with a Mithradatic woman, of whom it was said even to kiss her would bring death. In certain slants of light, with a little perspective, these sites become not so much gardens as adventures.

One of the most beautiful of these Renaissance gardens is the fountain-strewn garden of the Villa Lante in the little town of Bagnaia, about forty miles north of Rome. It was laid out in 1568 by Cardinal Gianfrancesco Gamara and ever since has been praised by garden critics and designers for its beauty and balance. Of all the great pleasure houses of Italy, Wharton wrote, the Villa Lante possessed the highest quality of garden-magic. Here, she believed, the garden surpassed the surrounding landscape; Lante was a garden to look into, not out from, as with many of the villa gardens she knew. It was the use of fountains here that earned the garden its praise. The builders used the abundant springs from the nearby Cimini Hills, which are rich in mineral waters and the site of ancient baths. The garden consists of three level terraces supported by tall retaining walls linked by slopes and a famous water chain, a long, descending line of basins that flows down through the center of steps connecting the terraces. Just outside this structured garden is a natural park, with long diagonal avenues, interspersed with one of the finest wooded bosques of any Italian garden.

As was often the case with these gardens, Villa Lante is laid out with a unifying metaphor, this one involving the Fall of Man. According to interpreters, the wilder bosque represents the golden age of innocence and nature's abundance, and the inner, more formalized and structured garden tells the story of the Fall, of original sin and the loss of innocence. According to the metaphor, after the Fall, nature no longer gives freely of her bounty, and human beings must now live by their intellect. The garden, with its water passages and fountains, represents the ingenuity of the intellect, and feeds the body and the soul. All this, presumably, is told by means of the linked terraces. Interestingly enough, even though the garden was the work of a cardinal, in true Renaissance form the story is told not through Christian metaphor but in classical imagery. At the uppermost level, the sky god Jupiter releases the Flood, the human race is swallowed, dolphins swim in woodlands, and Deucalion—the classical version of Noah—and his wife land on the high mount of Parnassus. Lower terraces relate the story of cultivation and harvests, and the third terrace, the most formalized, is a hymn to civilization. All this is very carefully worked out in mathematical formulas and architectural relationships, a progression toward formality, with the wild wood—one might even say the wilderness—left unstructured beyond the walls.

You could not tell any of this the first time I visited the Villa Lante. Italy was experiencing record cold and heavy snows that winter. The great water chain, although still running, was festooned with elaborate knobs of ice. The fountain of the river gods, representing the Tiber and Arno, was an icy cascade; the formal parterre at the lowest level, which contains a splendid fountain of Moors, was a streaming ribbon of ice; and the most important fountain of all, the pool with the fountain of Pegasus, had been transformed into an abstraction; you could hardly see poor Pegasus for all the ice. I dashed from fountain to fountain trying to avoid wind, and finally found a sunny balustrade sheltered from the wind where I settled down to make sketches of ice.

I couldn't complain though. The benign Roman spring was in the offing and a few days later the beds of pansies were in full bloom at the Villa Doria Pamphili just above Trastevere, a fine open park favored by Edith Wharton in her youth and now the haunt of Roman runners and dog walkers. The vast parklike gardens of the Villa Borghese were green and warm, and I spent a few comfortable days on benches of the Pincian Hill above the Piazza di Puopolo, where Wharton spent some of the happiest days of her childhood years playing with other children under a canopy of trees.

Boston at this time was locked in ice and snow, with a high wind and icicles hanging like prison bars from the back porch roof and my faux Italian garden a singular sheet of glaring crusted snow, all beds and allées, obliterated, and my spiky Italianate evergreens capped with snow and looking for all the world like the helmets of exotic warriors. I began to suspect that there was perhaps good reason why my mentor, Andrew Jackson Downing, had chosen to import the ideas of English garden design to the Northeast, rather than the fragile formality of the gardens of Italy.

5

The Genteel Romantics

CLEW: *I wish to inspire all persons with a love of beautiful forms, and a desire to assemble them around their daily walks of life. I wish them to appreciate how superior is the charm of that home where we discover the tasteful cottage or villa, and the well designed and neatly kept garden or grounds, full of beauty and harmony . . .*

Andrew Jackson Downing, *Victorian Cottage Residences*

Of all the labyrinths and mazes of the ancient world, the most famous, and the one that has lent its name to many maze traditions, was the Minoan labyrinth at Knossos on Crete. The structure may have existed in some form as early as 2000 B.C., and there is some indication that the Cretans may have borrowed the idea of a vast, internal, citylike maze from the earlier Egyptian labyrinth at Crocodilopolis at Lake Moeris.

The Cretan maze was essentially a complex of winding paths deep in the interior chambers of the walled city. Here the Minoans practiced the sport of bull leaping, which was an important aspect of the Minoan bull cults of the period. Young men and women would dodge or leap over the horns of a charging bull as a part of one ceremony. The bull, or Taurus, of King Minos is the origin of the story of the terrible Minotaur, who lurked in the depths of the maze. The word "labyrinth" is derived from this place; a *labrys* is a double-headed ax, and the interior rooms where the bull cult ceremonies would take place were called the House of the Double Axes. Here captives were trained for the dangerous bull leaping sport that gave rise to the legend of Theseus and the Minotaur.

According to the Greek myth, the maze at Knossos was designed by the craftsman Daedalus. It was an elaborate and complex series of paths, and once you got inside, you could not get out without a guide. In the center lived the Minotaur, a being with the body of a man and the head of a bull, or vice versa in some versions. In either form he had an insatiable appetite for human flesh. The Minotaur was the unfortunate offspring of Pasiphae, the wife of Minos, the king of Crete, who had coupled with a white bull.

The son of King Minos had been murdered by the Athenians and as retribution for this crime, Minos decreed that every nine years a tribute of seven young men and seven maids must be sent to Knossos for sacrifice. The young people were then sent into the labyrinth constructed by Daedalus to be eaten by the Minotaur. The king of Athens at this time was Aegeus, whose son was the hero, Theseus. Early in his heroic career Theseus offered to join the troop of young people sent off to Knossos and vowed to slay the monster and put an end to the tribute. Over his father's objections, he sailed off, but before leaving Athens, Theseus told his father that when the ship returned, if he had been victorious he would hoist a white sail. If he had lost, his crew would raise a black sail.

During the review of the sacrificial victims before the king at Knossos, Theseus was spotted by the king's daughter Ariadne and the two fell in love. Ariadne gave Theseus a sword and a ball of thread, and on the appointed day of the tribute, Theseus attached the thread to the entrance and entered the complex pathways of the labyrinth, working his way deeper and deeper through the dark hallways, spinning out the thread behind him. At the center of the maze he encountered the Minotaur and a great fight ensued. Theseus killed the Minotaur, followed the thread back out to the entrance, and then fled Crete, taking Ariadne with him.

The story has the sad ending of many of these mythological tales, however. Instructed by a dream, Theseus deserted Ariadne on the island of Naxos and sailed for home. But as he entered the harbor, he forgot his promise to signal and sailed in with the black sail raised, the traditional color of the sails of Greek vessels. His distraught father, believing his son dead, threw himself from a cliff, thus giving his name to the Aegean Sea.

There was more to come, though. The enraged Minos had Daedalus and his son, Icarus, imprisoned in his own labyrinth. Here, the ingenious Daedalus constructed wings with feathers and wax and the two flew off to freedom. But, even though he had been warned not to fly too high—or too low—the ecstatic young Icarus, with typical teenage exuberance, soared ever higher and came too close to the sun. The heat melted the wax that held the wings together, and he crashed into the sea and drowned.

Fortunately the garden mazes of our time have more pleasant associations. In fact, the ability to go for a long contemplative walk without ever leaving the confines of your property was one of the original intents of the early European gardens. From Roman times up to the late nineteenth century, the world at large was not an entirely safe, nor pleasant, walking ground, populated as it was in some sections by brigands, highwaymen, street ruffians, beggars, squalor, horse traffic, slop pails, and debris cascading down from upper-story windows. Carriage jams in Paris in the mid eighteenth century were said to be common. You could drive on either side of the street in those times, and two carriages would sometimes meet head on, and since neither could back up, other carriages entering the narrow streets would jam in behind them, resulting in an eighteenth-century version of road rage, complete with insults and sword fights.

Better to stay beneath the shaded lime bowers and flowering arbors of your grounds, or beside the quiet waters of a garden pool or fountain.

The rustic gardens of mid-nineteenth-century America had a similar purpose. The idea of the designers was to provide a place to walk in a safer, more comfortable version of the wilderness without ever leaving your own land. The main proponent and the prime American importer of this design idea was Downing, who began his career in the 1840s and from whose book I took the plans for my own house.

Downing was part of an antebellum landscape and literary movement called the Genteel Romantics, whose defining characteristic was a love of country life and nature, and a desire to refine America's manners and morals. Unlike the transcendentalists, with whom they shared some values, theirs was not necessarily a spiritual quest; the Genteel Romantics did not look to nature to provide metaphysical enlightenment, and they did not share the Thoreauvian love of wild nature. They merely took nature as entertainment, a pastime, an aesthetic to be appreciated mainly for its beauties.

Downing, who was the prime mover among the landscape gardeners of the group, was born in Newburgh, New York, in 1815. His father, who had been a nurseryman himself, died while Andrew was still young; an older brother took over the business and was soon joined by Andrew. Through their business they came to know the local gentry in the then fashionable Hudson River Valley region, where New Yorkers had laid out gardens and estate grounds overlooking the river. Andrew took over the nursery operation from his brother in 1837 and the following year began an upward social spiral. He married Caroline DeWindt, who came from a well-to-do family (she was the grandniece of John Quincy Adams), and then began writing magazine articles and books, the first of which was an article entitled "A Treatise on the Theory and Practice of Landscape Gardening, Adapted to North America."

As this title implies, Downing used European models of landscape design and altered them slightly for the American grounds. The ideas were borrowed, in the main, from Lancelot "Capability" Brown, an eighteenth-century English landscape architect who emphasized naturalistic landscapes—acres of trimmed lawns offset by groves of rounded trees and small hillocks, interspersed with glistening bodies of water. The idea was to provide a view of your landholdings from the terrace of the manor house, your private version of a carefully landscaped Eden. This is the landscape you still see today on the great estates of England—not the highly designed, trimmed, geometric gardens of France, nor the rooms and ilex-lined paths of the Italian garden, nor the small, intimate English cottage gardens—but great rolling sheep meadows and hilltop clusters of round-topped trees where rooks circle and call. Brown was all the rage in eighteenth-century England; he had earned his nickname from his ability to lay out a landscape, but in fact he swept away hundreds of old Renaissance-styled gardens in his desire to refashion estate grounds. You can still see the influence of his work here in America in the wide rolling greens and links of golf courses with their highly managed and manicured landscape of open ground and islands of trees, offset with small ponds.

Downing added to this English design the idea of a picturesque, wilder park, a heavily wooded terrain planted with larches and pines and cut by rocky outcroppings and gloomy, mysterious banks, with rustic woodland paths winding through them. Here, in these darkened paths, he allowed the mystery of wilderness to endure. On some still, autumnal evening, one might hear the scramble of goat hooves and sense, if only for a second, that some ancient hoofed god had been there. But this was, above all, a controlled chaos, wild in appearance but accessible. It had the superficial imagery of wilderness, including all the mystery, but none of the real dangers, like bears, snakes, and lost valleys or mountain slopes. It was meant to be a wilderness fit for ladies. In fact women were accepted, even enticed, to come into this environment. One of the main characteristics of the Genteel Romantics was that they encouraged women to go outdoors and enjoy gardening (not farming mind you, which was rough and unappealing), but walking, and flower collecting. This was the period when the impractical, but beautiful, American flower garden came into fashion, and women were invited to make forays into the woodlands to pick wildflowers and to collect mosses and arrange them and replant them on their own properties.

By the 1870s the influence of Downing's two books, *The Architecture of Country Houses* and *Victorian Cottage Residences,* had spread throughout America. There was not an estate ground in this country that did not in some way respond to his ideas, to the letter in some cases, and in reaction in a few. By the end of the century the ideas first introduced by Downing and company set in motion a whole series of American garden fashions that continue to this day. He was the most influential and inventive landscape designer of his time. Tragically, but true to Romantic form, Downing died young in a steamboat accident. The vessel had caught fire and

Downing was last seen on the upper decks throwing wooden chairs down to the struggling passengers who had jumped overboard. After his death, his protégé, Frederick Law Olmsted, took over and went on to become the acknowledged father of American landscape architecture.

Some of the influence of Downing and the Genteel Romantics, primarily the encouragement of women gardeners and the use of ornamental flowers, reached down to the middle class and even to the working class yards and gardens. The traditional yard of the post–Civil War period demonstrated their influence. It would have been characterized by Harrison's yellow roses and lilies of the valley, and on the shady north side of houses by ostrich ferns and lady ferns that the women would have brought home from their woodland forays. The middle-class town gardeners would have grown russet apples and maiden's blush damson plums and daylilies, and their flower beds were planted to old-fashioned single hollyhocks, sweet williams, pinks, and squills. The most famous American addition to garden design, the lawn, was yet to be born. Grass in these yards was scythed and rough; smooth lawns would not appear until the invention of the reel lawn mower later in the century. Homeowners may even have kept a horse tethered in the yard from time to time to crop the grass. The front of the house during this period was unplanted and generally unadorned, except perhaps for a white lilac by the front gate. Basically householders wanted to be able to see who was going by on the street; gardens were in back of the house, as they are in England to this day.

By the 1880s the yard had become more formalized, with star-shaped beds and a fountain in the front yard, and perhaps an iron statue of a deer. Dorothy Perkins roses were the rage during this time, but twenty years later, at the turn of the century, everyone was planting Lombardy poplars, spirea, and beds of Madonna lilies and delphiniums. Garden lecturers of the period advised suburban property holders to lay out a garden hose in a series of pleasing curves and do away with all the straight-running

---

flower beds of the past. They were also advised to construct rock gardens during this period, and if necessary to go out in the wild forest and look for interesting rocks to bring home.

By the 1920s, thanks to the influential work of Edith Wharton, and an earlier book by Charles Platt, the estate gardens of the rich took on an Italian face, with many pools and fountains and paths and statuary. These ideas soon filtered down to the middle class, and for a brief period, a decade or so, everyone was thinking in the Italian style, there was even a Boy Scout manual on how to design an Italian garden. But in the next decade the fashion of planting evergreens around a foundation in a sort of dot-dash system—one high and narrow for every low, rounded shrub— came into style and has more or less prevailed into our time. Lawns came into fashion at this time and all the hedges and the willows and the old shrubs and even the trees were severely clipped. By the 1950s, with the advent of power mowers, and more recently the hideous, polluting, energy-consumptive riding mower, lawns grew in size and overwhelmed the whole idea of "garden." Old shrubs and patches of berry bushes, even the overgrown corners of the yard, were cleared to make turning room for the ever-larger mowers. The time required for maintenance became a major element in landscape design. In spite of the so-called time-saving power tools—mowers, leaf blowers, hedge trimmers, chain saws, and the like—schedules did not permit the slow, heavy work of trimming and digging by hand, and the idea of a low-maintenance property came into vogue.

Fortunately, in the 1990s a new garden style began to emerge. This involved the use of native plants for ornamental purposes, smaller lawns, and flowing, naturalistic lines with wild, uncultivated, and unclipped corners to encourage shelter for local wildlife. Although there are now numerous books on the subject, including how-to manuals and magazine articles, the style is still not favored among the uniform, lawn-dominated suburbs and newer developments. In fact, some communities still have laws on their books against "noxious weeds," by which they mean the colorful wildflowers of fields and meadows such as hawkweeds, black-eyed Susans, Queen Anne's lace, dandelions, and daisies that "invade" lawns. There have even been a number of court cases in which towns have attempted to force gardeners to cut their untrimmed, "weedy" lawns. All of these changes in style need time to gain popularity, but it appears that, in spite of local regulations, the age of the shorn lawn is slowly waning and may eventually be replaced by the Medieval version of the flowering mead and the Italian *prato,* a rough, grassy area that permits, and even encourages, the blossoming of wildflowers.

Downing and the Genteel Romantics hoped to avoid, at all costs, the nastiness of reality. They had retreated to that region just beyond the suburbs, the so-called borderlands, where there were still farms and woods. Here they sought peace and quiet and beauty and civilization. They wrote poems to life in the country; they designed gardens for their estates that gave all the pleasures of outdoor life, such as wide vistas, easier walking paths, and intimations of wilderness, and none of the hardships of frontier life, or life in the crowded, squalid cities.

This idea suited my situation well, I thought. I did not have the scenic vistas of the Downing era estates, but the concept of laying out a rustic, mythopoeic landscape with farms to the east and west, and a dark wood to the north, seemed to fit the borderland environment in which we were living at that time—the wilder edge between the suburbs to the east and the countryside to the west. I wanted to build a house in the landscape, or rather a house of the landscape.

In English, the word "villa" generally means a large house in the country. In the original Latin it had more or less the same meaning, except that it included outdoor spaces such as the central courtyard. But in Italian, the *villa* includes the living quarters and the outdoor spaces around the dwelling, which is to say the terraces, walkways, parterres, flower beds, groves, and sections of wild native forest, as well as the lands beyond the gardens, with no one of these parts existing independently. During the Renaissance and baroque period, the grounds and the manor houses of the grand villas were designed and laid out by the architect responsible for the property. The gardens were not a secondary addition created by some expert who was called in after the house was constructed, they were an integral part of the whole. The use of a landscape architect, someone responsible for the design of the grounds alone, came later in history, around the eighteenth century, and was officially established as an art (or a science) by Olmsted, beginning in 1858.

Downing was a Renaissance-style designer. He was first a plantsman and later a house architect, so he was disinclined to think of house and grounds separately. Unfortunately, Downing and his ilk are now a rare breed, and when I went to lay out my house and grounds, I was on my own, even if I could have afforded to hire a twenty-first-century Renaissance architect. I did, however, have reprints of Downing's books, and from these I selected his design for a small timbered cottage, the sort of place where the groundskeeper for an Italianate villa might live, not by any means the grand manor. The house was overly built, far too heavy on the interior, and almost Elizabethan in structure, but on the outside it had the refined vertical lines and elaborate filigreed barge boards and decorative elements so favored by Mr. Downing and company—"an ornamental style such as would be suitable for a gentleman," as he phrased it.

Despite Downing's attention to details in the architectural planning of his country houses, such as heating and furniture, he did not concern himself overly with the siting of "necessary houses," as they were euphemistically called, nor with the necessities of plumbing (nor, incidentally, did Downing's Victorian contemporary Mr. Henry Thoreau in his detailed description of his house at Walden Pond). But health codes of our time have more than made up for any oversight in the nineteenth century, and the construction of septic systems seems to have become a major aspect of garden design. Where I live, state codes require the imposition of veritable Indian mounds of piled earth to ensure proper drainage.

To my horror, these codes required that I dig up practically the entire backyard to fit in the various drainage fields, tiles, and overflow drainage fields. This was for me, as it is for many house builders, a literal nightmare—worse so in my case since the one thing I fear, hate, loathe, abhor, and despise, and even have bad dreams about, is the bulldozer. It was bad enough when one appeared in my sanctuary to dig the foundation for the house. But the health inspector announced that in order to meet state health codes I would have to dig up my carefully planned garden beds This sent me into weeks and months of negotiations with various boards in an attempt to save my preexisting gardens. During this time, I traipsed from bureau to bureau, bundles of incomprehensible (to me) plans under my arm, seeking a proper authority to hold at bay the hideous machine.

But all to no avail. My alternative plans were rejected, and if I so much as deigned to suggest that rejection A was not valid because of water drainage patterns or soil samplings, I would be informed that it was in fact B that was the cause of the official rejection, whereupon I would tunnel through more bureaucratic chambers to prove to them that B was not a problem because A had taken care of B. Subsequently I would be informed that neither A nor B was the real problem. The real cause of the rejection was—C. And then I would learn, after weeks of work, that C was rejected because A was inadequate. It was as if I had somehow stumbled into a Kafkaesque web in which I did not know what crime I had committed, where the trial was to be held, and who to ask, or blame for, the mix-up. There were so many layers of bureaucrats in the process, speaking in so many tongues, that I could not comprehend enough to even fight them.

I couldn't complain though. I figured that this was some kind of karmic revenge. For years I had sided with the various labyrinthine health codes because they represented the last and sometimes the best defense against developments I was opposing.

In the end, on a dark day in autumn, the bulldozer entered my sanctuary, tore out hedges in one simple pass, ripped through beds of delphiniums that had taken years to establish, plowed all my carefully nurtured beds and parterres asunder, and dumped dry, sterile gravel on the ground, then covered the whole garden over again with a horrid yellow subsoil. The grunting beast chewed great rutted tracks here and there in the lawn, chipped tree trunks with its earth-stained blades, ruined yet more garden beds, drove over precious shrubbery, and unearthed enormous raw boulders, exposed them to the sun for the first time in ten thousand years, and then left them strewn around the boundary walls like dead rhinoceri.

So ended my first garden on that land.

I had lived lightly on the property for years, first in the old house with an illegal (no doubt) cesspool that was built sometime in the mid nineteenth century, and then for a while in the small studio I built myself, with a definitely illegal earth closet, another nineteenth-century device that functioned perfectly well, as far as I could tell, without the intervention of the bulldozer and upturned earth. For two years I had lived in the studio without electricity or running water and had heated the place with wood.

Now I was abiding by the written health codes of contemporary America and destroying land in the process. It was, to my mind, a little like the infamous American general of the Vietnam era who claimed that it was necessary to destroy a certain village in order to save it.

The gardens I had originally planned for the Downing-styled cottage were to be traditional Victorian gardens. Using *The Architecture of Country Houses,* I perused the plant lists and spent many rainy days meditating on how best to lay things out, and what would go where once I got the money together to call in someone with topsoil and trees and shrubs, and reshape this property into a proper estate grounds.

For a house in this style, Downing recommended that the grounds be rendered in an ornamental manner, in keeping with the exterior of the house. He suggested the growing of fruits of "a delicate kind" and vegetables of fine flavor, and believed that a total of one-third of the property should be used for a kitchen garden, the remaining for ornament. But the last thing he would want you to actually see from your terrace is this kitchen garden, so in his design he hid it behind a trellis grown with Chinese twining honeysuckle, trumpet vine, or sweet-scented clematis. In front of the trellis he recommended a little lawn, with walks leading around to the kitchen garden, which, as he made clear, should be surrounded with fruit trees.

Despite my best efforts, the money for this admirable garden design did not materialize, and so I plodded on in my peasant's way, digging beds myself, hauling topsoil around in broken wheelbarrows salvaged from the town dump, building compost piles, planting those few trees I could afford, where I could afford to dig them, and evolving the garden rather than planning it out and planting it in one purposeful burst of activity. It was years of work, and it never matched very closely the Downing designs, even though the house did.

This longer-range approach turned out to be a good thing, since long before this first garden plan for the house was anywhere near completed, I altered my ideas and began reshaping the garden in the Italian style. This one I intended to be permanent—no more new houses on the property and never again another septic system.

Along with a new house and garden, as a part of the Scratch Flat family accretion I began to accumulate children, furniture, rugs, books, cars, and stringed instruments (one extended family member was a guitar builder, another was a collector of antique ukuleles). Among these various and sundry items I inherited a Jack Russell terrier, who promptly adopted me as his primary ally in this life. He became my constant companion whenever I was outside, which was most of the time. If I went for a circuit walk to the hemlock grove, he was there, sometimes ranging out ahead of me in ever-widening gyres, sometimes tagging at my heels, and always poking his black nose into every hole, log hollow, rock crevice, tree crevice, leaf pile, brush pile, puddle, and pit he could find. He was also a constant presence in the garden. If I was in the process of digging a hole to plant a new tree, he would be standing beside me, ever at alert, his head cocked, watching my work intently. If I deserted this task and moved over to clip the maze, he would trot behind at my heels. And if ever I was on my knees with my hands deep in the good earth, about at his level in other words, I would hear his snuffling and glance over. There he was, eyes fixed on the ground, ears perked forward, ready for some action.

One day, some years after he adopted me, noting his constant vigil, I pointed to a stubborn root I was trying to extricate and gave him an order: "Attack" I said breathlessly.

This was the singular command he had been waiting for all these months and years. Without hesitation, he dove to earth and began digging furiously, and in a matter of seconds had excavated the recalcitrant root. I tried him on another root, with the same effect, and then another.

I learned that he would always dig on command, which was something that was no doubt imbedded in his rat-hunting genes long ago in rural England. He would also quit on command, and I learned that I could simply move down a garden row, ordering him to dig small holes, into which I could place whatever it was I was planting. This proved especially useful in autumn for planting bulbs, since the holes he dug were about right for daffodils and tulips. Furthermore, he had, I learned, the endearing habit of consuming with relish any cutworms or Japanese beetle grubs we turned up in the process of our various excavations, thereby saving me the nasty work of squishing them between my fingers.

This obsessive digging could easily have declined into a war between us, since his digging ability could just as easily have uprooted whole beds of flowers, but he had other obsessions in his small, dogly mind, namely, sticks. He would cruise the edges of the gardens or the woods and return with a suitably sized stick and cast it down in front of whomever was in the yard at the time, hoping to have it thrown, whereupon he would give chase. Having captured his enemy he would toss it in the air, kill it, and then bring it back and cast it down in front of the thrower again, staring at it all the while just in case it wasn't dead yet. Given a chance, he would do this all day, if anyone would throw the stick for him. But no one had the stamina to outlast him. Often, for lack of a thrower, he'd find a stick, carry it to the yard, and throw it for himself by tossing it up, catching it, killing it, and then tossing it up again—all day, every day.

His other work there was to protect the garden from intruders, which, in his mind, were legion. There were bears, wolves, foxes, ungulates, and all manner of unidentified species that lurked in the forest beyond the garden wall. I could not always see these, and I often wondered why, on some otherwise quiet afternoon, he would dash from the porch and race along the top of the stone wall barking furiously.

One afternoon, during lunch with a visiting maze expert, the dog leapt from his spot and charged out into the garden, sounding off with his usual ferocity.

"He always does that," I explained apologetically. "It's nothing, there's nothing there."

"You mean you don't see anything there," she said. "He does though."

"No, we used to follow him to see what he was after. There's never anything."

"Ah, but dogs can see fairies," she explained. "You must have fairies and sprites living out there in the woods."

This may or may not have explained his behavior. But there were true enemies that we could hear.

There is a lake over the hill behind the garden, and just beyond the lake on the west side there is a rail line. Trains passing a road at the north end of the lake sound off their whistles, and these evoke in our heroic guardian paroxysms of anger. Knowing that danger is close at hand, he'll charge out and patrol the entire property. Sometimes in winter he hears this enemy from inside the house and charges the door, leaping and barking until someone lets him out to attack.

This is actually excellent work he does, as my wife makes clear to me whenever I complain about his frantic behavior. No train has ever come into our yard, she points out.

On one occasion during an early spring walkabout I heard my assistant barking furiously in the woods beyond the wall. Nothing out of the ordinary really, except that he would return periodically to my side, circle my ankles and charge out again into alien forest to resume his barking, which I noticed had a slightly different, more frenetic (if that's possible) timbre to it. It occurred to me that he had treed something, and after a while I went out to see what it was. It turned out he was holding at bay the largest, wildest coyote I have ever seen.

Most of the coyotes that periodically cross this property are skittish things that tentatively climb over the walls to feed on compost. If they see you, or hear you, or even think they see you, they fade into the forest. But this animal was a monster, and he was standing his ground, a great gray and brown furred wolflike coyote, his forelegs on a low rock, staring back at this little canine *poseur* who circled at a safe distance yapping furiously. I was reminded of the scene in William Faulkner's story "The Bear" in which a fearless small dog had to be restrained from dashing into the swiping claws of the bear.

After a few seconds, it occurred to me that were he so inclined, this coyote could do away with my heroic guardian with a single bite, so I stepped forward and waved my arms. The coyote moved off indifferently and took a stand on another rock. The dog charged, circling and barking with even more ferocity, having presumed, I suppose, that he had got the better hand. But I called him off with a whistle and clapped my hands to scare off the intruder.

Several years back, on one of my rambles in a wooded area south of Scratch Flat, I stumbled onto a property that reminded me very much of the old landscape in which I had grown up. The property had a caved-in greenhouse, an abandoned carriage house, and just beyond it a sunken garden, rank with weeds. This was the environment of my childhood, redux. The garden was oddly situated, more or less in back of a seemingly uninhabited main house, almost out of sight actually, and with no apparent relationship to the main building. There were no descending stairs or terraces leading to the garden, as you would find in similar estates of the period, and yet the garden was clearly Italianate and was carefully designed. It was laid out on an east–west axis and was fairly narrow, only about thirty yards across. At the eastern end there was a terrace with a ruined pergola and arbor and what looked like an old fountainhead under the pergola. Below, down a short flight of cracked steps, was the sunken garden with a long, narrow reflecting pool in the middle, grown over entirely with waterlilies. The retaining walls on either side of the garden were fallen in at spots, the pool was half empty, and the green noses of huge bullfrogs protruded here and there among the lilies.

I went down the steps and walked along a weedy path toward the western end, where there was a small semicircular alcove with broken pillars just above the wall. In the alcove on a tall plinth was another moss-covered fountain with a waterspout emerging from the mouth of a human figure. The figure had a curling goatee, long ears, and horns. It was no less than my old friend Pan, here, yet again, in the civilized Boston suburbs.

I walked around the old weedy beds, and the frog pond, and terrace, imagining what it must have been like here in the years when this place was in flower. It was just the kind of environment I had come to love: ruined splendor, some great family in decline, complete with eccentric uncles, a passionate old gardening matriarch who hung onto the past, perhaps a chattering madwoman in the attic, many favored dogs buried on the grounds with extravagant pomp and circumstance, and a few remittance men, living abroad somewhere in the sad tropics.

It turned out that I was not too far off.

I then realized I was actually familiar with the house of which this garden was a part. It was "The Grange," a late-eighteenth-century Georgian structure owned by the Society for the Preservation of New England Antiquities. I had driven past the front of the property many times, but in my roadless wanderings in the woods behind the house I had never established exactly where I was in relation to the real world. I preferred to believe that I had stumbled onto a mythic, disappearing garden that would sink from the known world when I left, only to reappear when I took a certain path through the dark hemlocks.

The property had been established in the 1790s by John Codman. The estate was sold out of the family at one point, and then came into the family again in the 1860s when Ogden Codman, grandson of John, bought the place back and began to restore it. The Codmans developed an interest in landscaping. Ogden began collecting ornamental trees, and later in her life his wife, Sarah, in keeping with the vogue established by the Genteel Romantics, became a passionate flower gardener. Of the five Codman children, four never left home, one of these went crazy later in her life, and the fifth left the country and spent many of his years living abroad. In the late nineteenth century, and well into the twentieth century, this family continued its interest in gardening. In 1900, when the work of Charles Platt and Edith Wharton was coming into style, the matriarch had a garden in the Italian manner designed and planted behind the main house, the ruined garden into which I had stumbled.

Partly because it reminded me of the landscape of my youth, this particular Italian garden held a strange attraction for me. Sometimes I would carry lunch to the bench at one end of the garden and sit in the sun and eat and watch the frogs in the dark waters under the lilies. And sometimes I would return at dusk, when the shadows from the trees to the west cast a darkness over the whole sunken, still space, and the sky above the trees and the gardens took on a deeper shade of blue, and pink, with shredded ribbons of cloud stretched overhead. It had all the mystery of some forgotten corner of the world, where things might happen, where, as I often imagined, old John Codman the elder would shuffle out from the main house and engage me in a philosophical discussion, or Pan would come down off his plinth at the dark end of the frog pool and dash off into the wildwood for a Walpurgis Nacht romp.

One day, up behind the gardens, half buried in the earth and covered over with rotting leaves, I found the sculpted capitals of some of the pillars that once surrounded the terrace at the west end of the garden where Pan held sway. I thought these would make a fine addition to my emerging Italianate garden and searched out the caretaker for the place to ask what the fate of the capitals was to be. He told me that they were going to be used as part of the restoration of the garden, and true to form, a year or so later the gardener began to clean out the beds and patch up the walls and the sides of the reflecting pool. Slowly, season by season, he began to replant the beds, and over the years the architectural restoration of the garden proceeded.

Not long after I began following Edith Wharton in her travels around Italy I came across her book *The Decoration of Country Houses*. She had written it with a man named Ogden Codman, an old friend, or at least acquaintance of hers. It turned out that the man who laid out the Italian garden in Lincoln in 1899 was none other than Ogden Codman, Jr., the oldest son of Ogden Sr. and Sarah Codman.

Unlike his younger brothers and sisters, he had left home and moved to Paris and eventually became a respected New York architect who traveled in the same circles as Wharton. He designed many of the newer houses of the turn-of-the-century rich, including, I later learned, some of the brownstones in the town in which I grew up.

My dream of creating an Italian garden suddenly seemed part of some kind of karmic process.

6

Italian Reveries

CLEW: *The traveller returning from Italy, with his eyes and imagination full of the ineffable Italian garden-magic, knows vaguely that the enchantment exists; that he has been under its spell, and that it is more potent, more enduring, more intoxicating to every sense than the most elaborate and glowing effects of modern horticulture. . .*

Edith Wharton, *Italian Villas and Their Gardens*

Italy seems to have been destined by geography to be the conduit for the transformation of ideas from the ancient world to the modern world. This was no less true of gardens and mazes than it was for art and architecture. The earliest Christian mazes originally evolved in Italy and were based on the ancient Roman and classical labyrinth patterns that had been in use as a design form on the Italian peninsula since the Etruscan period.

Most of the earlier labyrinth designs in churches were small. The maze at Ravenna, which dates from A.D. 530, is only twelve feet across; there is a five-foot-wide labyrinth composed of porphyry and yellow and green marble in the church of Sta. Maria in Aquiro, in Rome; and another small maze graces the floor of the quiet little out-of-the-way church of Sta. Maria da Trastevere in Rome, a stone labyrinth of nine courses, about eleven feet across, which was constructed of colored marbles alternating with dark and light.

The point of all of these early Christian mazes was to recreate the journey of the pilgrim. Many of the larger church labyrinths were meant to be walked on. You followed the courses to the center without stepping across lines or walking straight onto the middle—which at some points during your labyrinth walk may be no more than a few feet away. As you walked this meandering, curving path you were supposed to meditate on life's journey, namely, the path to divine salvation. While walking, you emptied your mind of everyday thoughts and concentrated on the Divinity. It was, in essence, a walking meditation, a device popular in ancient and current theological practices, a means of acquiring insight.

The idea of the journey or pilgrimage to a sacred center occurs in all religions, although which form of enlightenment, or divinity, you encounter at the end or during the course of the journey depends on the pilgrim. You could gain knowledge of the Christian God, a flash of Nirvana, a purification of the soul—or, for that matter, an encounter with Pan and the untamed forces of wild nature. In all of these situations, what you gain by walking the maze is an experience of something that is beyond yourself, some transcendent encounter with the sublime beyond the everyday and human events. This is the same thing Thoreau spent so much of his life's journey seeking—a means of contact, although I daresay Thoreau would not stoop to admit that such insight could be attained in so structured an environment as a hedge maze, much less a pseudo-Italian garden.

There are certain times, usually early in the morning, walking my own labyrinth, when I think I glimpse a flash of some ancient, abiding force in the controlled, organized spaces of my garden. Partly this may arise from thinking of nothing in particular while I am walking, only to be jolted to my senses so abruptly that I can't quite establish my position in the world. At these moments I don't know where I am exactly and I don't know which way to turn in order to get out. With a little imagination I could be lost forever.

The most celebrated of the Medieval church labyrinths is the maze on the floor of the cathedral at Chartres: it is a large circle, forty-two feet across, with eleven courses and a unicursal route laid out in white paving stones, separated by black dividers. According to old documents and plans, there was once a stone at the center of this labyrinth, and on this stone there was carved a pagan image depicting Theseus and the Minotaur.

This idea of something dangerous lurking at the center of a labyrinth has roots that predate even the old story of Theseus and the Minotaur. The myth of a horned figure dwelling in the center of a sacred grove goes back as far as the Neolithic period. In some of these traditions the god or goddess was dangerous and had to be defeated in battle. Pan, of course, was a horned grove dweller himself, although decidedly more benign, even though he could be a troublemaker. But after Knossos, the story of a monster at the center of a maze was set down in writing and became a part of Western cant. There was a garden maze at Pompeii, for example, with a sign at the center: *Hic habitat Minotaurus.*

One of the better known of the older mazes in England was the twelfth-century hedge maze at Woodstock, planted by Henry II, the husband of the fiery queen Eleanor of Aquitaine. Henry's maze was a complicated series of paths, probably architectural, although later accounts suggest it was made of evergreens. He and a lady named Fair Rosamund began a clandestine affair, and the two would meet secretly in the innermost recesses of his complicated labyrinth. Rumors of this affair reached the queen. She obtained a clew, found her way through maze courses, and confronted Fair Rosamund. Always known for her ruthless practicality and logic, Eleanor presented Rosamund two possible alternatives—a dagger to the heart, or a bowl of poison. Poor Rosamund chose the bowl of poison and died therein.

By the Tudor period, this tragic, romantic story had become a favorite theme of poems and ballads, the best known of which was "The Life and Death of Rosamund, King Henry the Second's Concubine, And how she was Poysoned to Death by Queen Elenor." It is said that gossipy old Samuel Pepys had a copy of this ballad in his collection.

By the seventeenth century, the humane designs of the Italian gardens began to appear in France, where they were expanded and reshaped into highly geometric patterns. These French gardens, the grandest of which were constructed under the influence of the architect André le Notre, were vast symmetrical, mathematical, outdoor spaces, some of which reached from chateau to the horizon. And here once again the old labyrinthine design reasserted itself in the form of the puzzle mazes created from hedging material. These green interiors were at a far remove from the ancient temple labyrinths of Minos, which were rife with ritual symbolism; they were essentially pleasure gardens, entertainments, where the aristocracy played. But at their heart, the old idea of getting lost in wildness, the possibility, however remote, of danger, still existed.

There is a tiny maze, only a foot or so across, set on a wall outside the doors of the cathedral at Lucca. This maze, like the Christian maze at Chartres, has an image of Theseus and the Minotaur at the center, but for seven hundred years now people have been following the course of the labyrinth with their fingers and have obliterated the image. I discovered it while my wife was inside the cathedral on her quest for images of the Annunciation, and I too traced the paths with my own finger just to continue the tradition.

This was another one of those cold comfort trips to Italy (I have the bad habit of traveling to Italy in winter and invariably get stuck in freak cold spells). For some reason I seemed unable to get warm even in the benevolent month of March. I found myself losing all ambition. Finally, one night in Rome, in a dank pension room I realized why. I was ill with some odd recurring fever that gave me chills.

Hoping to bask out the sickness, we went farther south and settled in an empty hotel in Sorrento. Here, baking on the terrace set high above the bay in the warming sun of March, I recovered somewhat and forged on, ending up on the heights of Anacapri at the old villa gardens of Tiberius, restored by the eccentric Swedish doctor Axel Munthe in the early 1900s.

Munthe had studied in Paris with the neurologist Jean-Martin Charcot at La Salpêtriere and then had moved to Rome, and somehow worked his way in with the luminaries and aristocrats of his time. If you can believe his book, he was friends with nearly everybody in the Western world—the king of Sweden, Capresi peasants, Henry James, despicable Neapolitan bandits, and beautiful European aristocrats with hothouse temperaments. Like a true northerner, Munthe was obsessed with light and used to spend time on Capri seeking the sun. One afternoon, among the Roman ruins

on the heights of Anacapri, he was visited by a dark figure from an indeterminate period of history who said—in so many words—upon this rock
build your house.

Munthe spent the rest of his life restoring the Roman villa of Tiberius
that once stood on the heights. He was a skilled, if somewhat offbeat, doctor who did not charge the poor, who rescued stray dogs and injured birds,
and who was given to taking constitutionals with his entire menagerie—
dogs, birds, and his favorite, a recovering alcoholic monkey named Billy,
who he had saved from a cruel, drunken master. Munthe had a way of
ending up in the worst places at the worst times—Naples during the
cholera plague, Messina during the 1908 earthquake. He died in 1948 at
the age of ninety-two, a beloved expatriate, an egalitarian humanist, an
animal lover, and an early conservationist.

His memoir, *The Story of San Michele*, was first published in 1929 and by
the 1930s it was a best-seller, translated into forty languages. Now it is all
but forgotten, and having discovered it among a thousand other old
books in my parents' home, I had no idea whether it was still read or
whether the good doctor Munthe was even known in Anacapri. Not only
was he known, it turned out, he had evolved into a veritable local saint. I
met a man in the town square who had actually known Munthe. He had
been treated by him when he was a child of nine or ten, and when I mentioned Munthe's name he spoke in low, reverential tones. He told me the
good doctor regularly refused payment from the locals for his work.

I expected Anacapri to have changed for the worse—most places have,
after all. But in comparison to some of the old photos taken by Munthe
and his associates, Anacapri has gotten better. The bare, goat-tormented
hills have grown in, thanks primarily to Munthe. He worked tirelessly to
get the locals to stop slaughtering the great immigrations of quail that
come there every year, and the prohibitions have endured, for part of the
area is now a bird sanctuary and there is an anomalous Swedish and Ital-

ian ornithological station at the villa. On the unconstructed slopes below the village, the *macchia*, the thickets of holly oak, and the olives and myrtles are lush and bird loud. Every spring great flights of golden orioles, redstarts, flycatchers, and wheatears fly in from Africa. The villa itself, sundrenched, wine-soaked, and under constant construction in Munthe's time, has been maintained as a museum, a sort of memorial shrine to the great *dottore*.

I was there before the migrants returned, but in the garden the wisteria was in bloom, mixed with tulips and hyacinths, and no one was at the villa save a sleepy concierge. The place had a dreamy, idle quality to it: stone walkways, whitewashed walls, polished floors, the smell of cats, the elegant, albeit eclectic, statuary collected by Munthe.

In the early chapters of *The Story of San Michele*, Munthe claims that the spirit who encouraged him to settle at San Michele had also influenced the emperor Tiberius.

Tiberius was the stepson of Augustus, who had ruled successfully over the peaceful Roman Empire at the time of the birth of Christ. Once he assumed power, Tiberius grew paranoid and began killing his myriad suspects. In the end he became so suspicious of everyone that he threw it all off and retreated to Anacapri, where he built his villa, intending to live out the rest of his days there. He left Rome in the charge of a worthless sycophant named Sejanus. This pretender to the throne very soon calculated that if Tiberius were dead then he, Sejanus, would become emperor, and with this in mind he began scheming to kill the emperor. He was discovered in this plot and was summarily put to death, while in the meantime, languishing on the heights of Anacapri, poor old Tiberius grew ill. Hearing of this, the madman Caligula prepared to take over the empire, even before the emperor was dead. Tiberius experienced a recovery, however, and Caligula trembled for his life, until the servants of Tiberius solved the problem by smothering him on his sickbed. His villa fell into ruins and languished for fifteen hundred years until Munthe came along and took up the spirit of the place on his offer and stayed on to restore it.

One afternoon on the heights I dozed off on a bench in the garden. In my dazed, fevered sleep, I had visions of all this. Figures out of a dim past emerged and faded in my mind's eye. I heard the chirps of birds in the gardens, a cricket called; below, on the slopes, someone began shouting in the local dialect and then in the next breath broke into *bel canto* singing. A thousand feet below, a one-lung fishing boat chugged out to sea. Someone close at hand coughed and I woke up with a start. There, before me on the parapet, in front of a Sphinx statue, I saw a tall, bespectacled figure dressed in turn-of-the-century summer whites, his stiff collar loosened. He had a small white dog and a dark clipped poodle at his heels, and, at the far end of a long leash, a straining monkey with a curling tail was busy hunting grubs in the flower beds. I resolved to return to Sorrento to find a doctor.

Slightly recovered once more, I began ranging around the various gardens of the south of Italy. I went down the coast to Ravello and spent a couple of afternoons at the Villa Cimbrone and the Villa Rufolo, which is one of the oldest surveying palazzos in Italy, having been constructed sometime in the thirteenth century. The site was used as the setting in one of Boccaccio's stories from *Il Decamerone,* and Richard Wagner is reported to have been inspired here to write certain difficult scenes that he was struggling with in the opera *Parsifal.* I stayed with my affianced in a local pensione, aptly named La Casa d'Amore, and every day we walked around the town to either of the two gardens there. Here, in a cafe one day, we met a fellow sufferer, an odd American fellow with a bald head and bad cold. He was himself an avid gardener, a garden designer, he claimed, who had been offered, so he said, the job of head gardener at La Pietra, Lord Acton's garden in Florence. He said he had declined the offer so that he could devote his time to his painting.

"You're a painter as well as a gardener and a landscape architect?" I asked.

He sneezed bravely.

"I am indeed. I was invited to exhibit in the best New York galleries. But I have declined. I only wish to paint shepherds tending their flocks amidst ruins," he said. "And now, of course, such things are not *à la mode*." He sniffled. "No one wants my greater work, my sheep landscapes, my carefully rendered *paysages*. Only abstractions, constructions, installations."

He blew his nose, and then entered into a coughing fit.

I sympathized with him.

Somehow at this point we got onto the subject of Amazons.

"Yes, yes, yes," he said, impatiently, "I know all about Amazons. I am an authority on the shield of Athena."

I thought, finally, he had picked the wrong person to say this to and we would trap him in his lies, since Jill had just completed a research paper on the shield of Athena, which depicted a battle of the Athenians and Amazons. She was up to her ears in Amazons.

It turned out he did know a lot about Amazons.

He also knew a lot about Andrew Jackson Downing. He came from some upstate town in New York where there were many Downing-styled houses. He also knew all about the garden at the Villa Cimbrone, which was purchased and restored in 1904 by Lord Grimthorpe, an eccentric Englishman who had the gardens replanted in a strange mix of Edwardian and Italian garden styles. I was under the mistaken impression that the English writer Vita Sackville-West had had a hand in the design of the gardens here. I said as much.

"Oh no, no, no, no, my good man," he said, wagging his finger at me, "Vita never laid out a single garden in Italy. Only England. Dear old England."

He said this as if he had known Vita personally.

At Caserta, the great Versailles-like estate commissioned by Charles III, my fever returned. Caserta is one of the largest gardens in Europe, two miles all told, with a singular mile-long swath leading up to a famous waterworks with a statue of Actaeon the hunter, who was changed to a stag and then torn apart by his own hounds by way of punishment for having come across Artemis and her handmaidens bathing naked in a wild pool. Fortunately, this garden is so vast that the considerate management provides a little motorized tram to carry tourists up to the main fountain, which is supplied by water from distant mountains some thirty miles away. Normally I would have eschewed such conveniences, but in my weakened state I welcomed the ride and sat lolling in the back seat while we passed the splendors of Charles III and Bourbon Italy. I was, I am sorry to say, completely indifferent. I was more interested in a small coffee stand near the fountain to which I proceeded and commenced to order double espressos to see if I could revive my flagging spirits. Somewhat renewed, I wandered over to the great waterworks depicting the Actaeon and Artemis story. As with so many gardens, this first in a series of fountains at Caserta was part of a continuing metaphor, this one illustrating the savage state of man.

This was in March, nothing was functioning; the fountain was turned off, and workmen in bright orange boots were wading around in the pool with nets, catching huge carp and putting them in buckets—a far better show, I thought, than the full *cascata*. At one point an argument broke out among the workers, the nature of which I could not determine. Everyone was shouting at everyone else—something about fish and nets. In the midst of this, the apparent leader of the fishing expedition, a heavyset man, advanced on another worker and, his net raised, slipped and went over backward. This ended the battle. The various combatants were so consumed with laughter they forgot what the fight was about.

I asked the man at the coffee stand what the turmoil was over.

"Nothing at all," he said. "The boss always wants people to do things his way. Everybody's got a better way. That's all. Just like a government anywhere."

That night we returned to Sorrento and I dreamed of golden fish, Artemis unclothed at a fountainhead, and the hounds of Actaeon. By morning the weather had warmed, and just off the room where we were staying there was a little terrace, perched over the Bay of Naples. Colors were still feverishly vivid, all greens and blues, and rich, gray brown rock cliffs. In my morning siesta I dreamed of oranges and lemons. The sea below the terrace seemed a thousand miles distant.

That afternoon, with my affianced as conductor, I was shepherded up to the little town of Sant'Agato, where there was a small chapel associated with a monastery, the site, she hoped, of yet another obscure Annunciation. From a height in this town it was said that you can look down upon the two great bays of southern Italy, the Gulf of Salerno to the south and the Bay of Naples to the north.

We had coffee in a little square, and I found a place in the sun to rest while Jill went to the post office to ask about the monastery. Children were playing on swings in a school yard across from my selected spot, and while I sat there watching them an old dog wandered over and curled up at my feet as if he had known me all my life.

I greeted him in English and got no response. So I tried Italian. Still no response.

"Oh, but I understand, old man," I said. "You are but a poor old dog, and I am a weary, feverish traveler. But we do what we can, you and I. You rest here awhile. You must have been born here, between these two bays, spent your puppyhood here, and now time has caught up with you and you'll die here on these heights, whereas I will recover and travel on to parts unknown while your old bones rest in this spot. But I imagine you've been a good dog in this life and no doubt, when your time comes, your soul will soar aloft to dog heaven and the god of good dogs will fold you in his forelegs, and . . . "

As I was apostrophizing the old uncomprehending dog in this manner, I happened to look up. Two old ladies in kerchiefs on the other side of the street had halted midstride and were staring at me, aghast.

I shrugged apologetically and felt the fever return to my forehead.

Later, propelled forward by my ever-exploratory partner, we climbed a little hill toward a monastery where we could get a good view of the bays. It was an easy slope that mounted through umbrella pines and small cultivated fields, interspersed with lemon groves, but I was shuffling slowly and having to rest every few minutes. We could see the monastery bell tower at the top of the hill.

"Only a little farther. Come on then," she said.

"You go on," I said, "I'll just die here in Italy, happy at last."

She waited. I did not die, and we proceeded a little farther.

By the time we reached the top of the hill I was out of breath. Then I saw ahead of me a mystic sign.

Throughout all of these garden explorations, quite naturally, I had been thinking about American wilderness, about the sense of freedom that you are supposed to feel when you get out in the wilds, and about the fact that over the last few years grand vistas of mountains, rushing streams, waterfalls, soaring golden eagles, open ranges, and big, wild animals such as buffalo, Dall sheep, mountain goats, and antelopes had inspired no feeling whatsoever in me, not half the spirit, for example, as the discovery of evil-eyed Pan in some obscure garden corner. This realization, this apostasy of a former wilderness buff, this betrayal, is not a popular view among American environmentalists. I was afraid even to mention my lack of inspiration to allied conservationists; my appreciation for the ordered world of the Italian garden was a form of love that dared not speak its name among such people. And then, here, on this height between the two great bays of southern Italy, in the ancient landscape of Pan, I saw a sign, a mystic vision, a cosmic pronouncement.

On the wall of the monastery, in old, much faded Latin lettering, were the prophetic words out of Isaiah.

"*Vox clamatis ad Deserto*"

A voice crying in the wilderness.

What can this mean? I asked my companion. It seemed that the message, painted there some four hundred years ago, was written for me. My head was swimming.

"It means nothing," she said. "You need more coffee is what it means."

That night, back in Sorrento I had another bizarre dream that seemed to last the night long. The dream was so real it was almost a vision, and various scenes from this epic played and replayed over and over again. The basic plot involved a great ranging battle, fought on green rolling fields between bosquey dells, in a landscape such as might have been designed by Capability Brown himself. The scenario involved a war between strange, boar-headed Mongol warriors on fast little ponies and white crusader knights on more stately, slower horses. All night the armies clashed to and fro across the green fields. The knights charged down across the meadows, driving the boar-headed men back into the forest. Then from another quarter, a densely packed Mongol horde would sally forth from the trees on their little ponies to drive the knights back across the field. After a nightlong battle, it appeared that the boar-headed men were getting the upper hand. Then in a dreamy dawn, the filtered cloudscape parted and a veritable battalion of Amazons burst out of the sky on horseback and showered a rain of arrows down upon the Mongols, driving them back into the bosque on their speedy little ponies and ending the battle.

That morning my fever broke.

Into the Wild

CLEW:

The land is the Garden of Eden before them, and behind them a desolate wilderness.

Joel 2:3

Woe unto them that join house to house, that lay field to field, till there be no place, that they may be placed alone in the midst of the earth!

Isaiah 4:5

A year or so after I planted my maze I happened to meet a labyrinth designer named Marty Cain and invited her to come up and walk my invention. Immediately she remarked on the alignment of the maze and the fact that I had laid out this labyrinth perfectly with the cardinal points. As at Ravenna, it is divided into four quarters, and the quarters match the rising and setting sun of the spring equinox—give or take a few days in either direction. This was in fact an accident, but as Ms. Cain suggested, there are no accidents when it comes to this sort of thing. "The maze comes from the heart," she said. "You can't do it wrong."

Mazes and labyrinths are very much in fashion now. There seems to be a renewed interest around the world in the rediscovery of their ancient spiritual powers, as well as their architectural structure in formal garden designs. A few years ago, the English Tourist Board established the Year of the Maze, partly in recognition of the turf maze as a part of the national heritage of the British Isles, and recently in the Americas, New Age followers, churches, and even those working with the concept of healing gardens have been constructing mazes. One of the best known in this renaissance of mazes is the labyrinth in Grace Cathedral in San Francisco, which was laid out by Lauren Artress, the Canon for Special Ministries.

Artress had learned of the ancient faith in the spiritual power of the labyrinth and, having experienced this force on her own in a church maze, she constructed one for the cathedral floor. She used the design of one of the best known of all the medieval labyrinths, the stonework design in the floor of Notre Dame de Chartres.

The maze at Chartres was probably completed about the same time as the cathedral, in 1260, but when Artress and her friends first went there to research the design and walk this sacred path, she found the whole thing covered over with chairs. She and her fellow Americans had to go around moving chairs out of the way so they could see the structure and walk it.

It was clear, once the new labyrinth at Grace Cathedral was completed, that Artress had struck a harmonic chord in the American mind. The San Francisco labyrinth has become so popular that it has evolved into a veritable pilgrimage site on its own. To capitalize on this, and to encourage the spiritual and (some argue) the physical health benefits of walking a labyrinth, the church prepared model kits that can be used to create your own maze.

But quite apart from the religious aura of the maze, labyrinths seem to be experiencing a major renaissance partly because they are simply fun to walk. Some have been laid out in cornfields in the American Midwest, there's a huge one in New Jersey, and another on a farm in central Massachusetts, and they are regaining fashion in the gardens of France and England. Some of these are cut on the lawns of churches, some built of stone in suburban backyards, and some are cut into cornfields each season and are so complicated that flags and guides are needed to thread your way through them. A few of these have been constructed with odd building material. Marty Cain, as part of a restoration project undertaken by Boston area artists, once built a labyrinth out of turkey feathers.

I was blissfully unaware of this revival when I first thought to lay out a maze in my garden. I'm not sure why I liked them, except that I liked very much the idea of a structure created by plant material, and I also liked the idea of getting lost in your own backyard. Even after I began researching labyrinths I was unaware of the fact that anyone else was actually doing this sort of thing. Then one day I stumbled onto a maze created from hay bales on the quadrangle of Wheaton College in Norton, Massachusetts. It turned out to be the handiwork of Marty Cain, who had an exhibit of her stoneworks at the college gallery at the time. A few months later, by one of those weird coincidences that seemed to have evolved around the construction of my own labyrinth, I happened to meet her. Since she was interested in earth mounds and earth art, I subsequently invited her to investigate a serpentine earthworks I knew about at a nearby site that was held to be sacred to the Native American people who lived in the region.

———

On one visit to my garden, Cain told me that the trees at the center of my maze should be growing with far more vigor than those on the outer edges. "It's where the energy source lies," she explained, "the spiral concentrates the power and the plants respond. So does the soul."

The trees in my maze were mere slips at this stage; if you chose, you could walk through them to the goal without bothering to tread the full length of the courses. But after three growing seasons, I noticed that she was right. The trees in the center, having received no more attention than any of the other trees in the maze, were much more vigorous than those elsewhere in the circles. It made me wonder whether I had gotten in over my head with this maze business.

The planting of this maze was the first serious tree planting I had undertaken on the property. My earliest garden here consisted mainly of vegetables and a few annuals. In the following years I added a few perennials, then I began planting shrubs, and then for about three years I grew roses, which turned out to be a total failure. They blossomed in all their rosy glory the first year, and then, except for a few varieties, which I still have, began languishing in subsequent seasons so that after three or four years they were reduced to little thorny shrubs that threw out a few shriveled blossoms each year in June and then declined over the course of the season, victim to the legion of pests that affect roses. One year I recognized this pattern and dug them all out.

Once the maze was established I began to collect trees. I started with the common species, dogwoods, firs, hemlocks, then ornamental species such as katsura, weeping beeches, laburnums, pagoda trees, styrax, and tree lilacs. Some of this tree planting involved filling in grassy patches that I had originally meant to leave open, and once these were filled up, I had to start clearing back more brushy land that I had purposefully left in the corners of the gardens. These sections of the property were fine greeny tangles in summer and autumn, but by November they always took on a desolate, gray brown facade. So I replanted them with shrubs and trees that held green longer into the bleak midwinter. Slowly, over the years, the barren-ground landscape began to take on a deeper green, a kinder, more humane face than the sere November to April visage that characterizes most of the landscape in the region. My land began to remind me—in a much diminished form—of a property I had worked on just before I moved to Scratch Flat.

For a short while, a matter of months, I had lived as the caretaker for what are now the public gardens of Polly Hill on Martha's Vineyard. I was really only house-sitting there, but from time to time trees would be dropped off and I was instructed by phone where to place them. I knew absolutely nothing of tree planting; the extent of my gardening experience at that time was vegetable growing and the little yard work I used to do for old man Brunton, plus one short stint setting out young conifers with Charlie Parsons in the Great Forest. But as instructed, I went out and dug the holes, prepared them as I was told, and then set out the trees. Polly Hill herself, "the Lieutenant" as the local tradesmen used to call her, was never one for effusive compliments, but I do remember her one day telling me that I had done fair work setting out her crab apple trees, "only a *little* crooked," she said. I learned later that I should take this comment as the equivalent of a papal blessing.

Years after, many years after, when her land opened as a public arboretum, I went back and visited the grounds. It was here, wandering around the property with my daughter, who was a student of botany at the time, that I came to appreciate the enduring qualities of ornamental trees. There, growing in the open ground near some boxwood hedges, I saw the flowering crab, *Malus torringaides,* that I had planted twenty-five years earlier. I went around the property and made a little list of the different varieties that were growing there and then that winter filled out an order at a plant nursery. When the trees came in the spring, having prepared, à la Polly

Hill, a site for them the autumn before, I planted them in the ground. God only knows, given the rate of development around here, what these trees will look like twenty-five years from now. The act of planting trees is nothing if not a statement about place, an intention.

My old friend Charlie Parsons was periodically sent out from his known territory within the Great Forest to plant trees in those regions cut over by the state. He never liked this work, he told me. He was more of a wood cutter than a wood planter, but although he himself may not have said as much, it seemed to me that his real pleasure, and perhaps one of the reasons he had ended up in this line of work (quite apart from the fact that this was the only employment possibility in the area), was that he enjoyed walking around in the forest every day. Charlie really was the sort of old-fashioned woodsman from the time of Teddy Roosevelt and John Burroughs and Ernest Thomson Seton. He and his type were the front line of the American westward expansion. The good peasantry of Europe, those who lived in the deep country and cut wood and hunted and even foraged for wild plants such as mushrooms to supplement their diet, were essentially cultivators.

Charlie would have none of that. With his woodcutting skills, and the amount of land he had to work with—vast by European standards—he could have cleared an acre or two, planted a crop of potatoes and beets, grown his spinach and lettuce, raised a hog or two and chickens, and stored enough food to last a winter. But that was not Charlie's way. His relationship with the world was more that of the hunter, and whatever plant-gathering abilities he had were more closely related to medicine than to food. He knew about hemlock tea and spruce gum, and a few other folkloric remedies. His primary food source was deer, supplemented in autumn by grouse and hare, and an occasional slab of bear meat, which was generally given to him by his bear-hunting friend down the road. Other than this wild game, his food supply was "boughten," as he called it, canned beans and peaches, milled flour for Elizabeth's sickening Norwegian pound cakes, and a vast supply of a canned product called "Spaghetti O's," a favorite food, I believe, of his overweight daughter Mary and his grandson Zeus.

Charlie's old bear-hunting friend, from whom I used to buy my rabbits, indicated to me in one conversation that Charlie was actually not that skilled a hunter. It was not so much the hunt, my informant told me, as getting enough deer or hare to last him through the winter. "After that, old Charlie just walks around with a gun, looking at things. Pokes around. Not serious like."

On those occasions when I went out in the woods with Charlie I did notice that he was overlooking a lot of plant food in his wanderings, whereas I was learning more and more about the edible wild plants of the region, and the more I wandered in Charlie's footsteps, the more plants I found. This was especially true in autumn when the mushrooms came into their season and the tubers of the groundnuts began to fill out.

After a year or so, I began to see the natural world as a version of some European town market where vegetables, chestnuts, olive oil, game, greens, cheese, sausage, and fruit all appear in the stalls at their appointed seasons only. I remember watching carefully for the proper setting of the elderberries, which I would pick to make elderberry wine, and I remember a constant vigil over the condition of a clump of groundnuts I found not far from Hurricane Brook, below Charlie's house. I was waiting for them to grow more and larger tubers before I harvested them.

This attention to the condition of wild plants alerted me to the condition of the weather. I worried during prolonged droughts; I waited for the autumn rains to bring up the mushrooms; I waited for the breakup of the ice in early March to bring up the skunk cabbage—the first edible green, something I actually tried only once—it had a sour cabbagelike flavor and you had to change the cooking water so many times it probably had absolutely no nutritional value. This quest for food also got me out on the land, away from the house, so that I came to know the comings and goings of the local mice, the arrival and departure of migratory birds, the resting place of local deer herds, the scratching trees of bears, and the handiwork of foxes and other predators. Once I found the half-buried carcass of a deer, and a nearby scat of what appeared to me from my book learning to be that of a mountain lion. I reported this excitedly to Charlie. "You bet," he said, "you got your catamounts all over these woods."

One September, after the rains, was particularly memorable. The mushrooms were sprouting all through the forest, the berries and the roots and tubers were ripe and full, birds were on the move, you could hear them passing at night, and in contrast to the stillness of August, there was a touch of excitement in the air, as if something was about to happen—which, of course, it was. Winter was on its way.

We had houseguests with us at this time, an intensely intellectual couple from our former lives in New York, who were on vacation and wanted a taste of wildness. It was my friend, Dr. Martini (he had a Ph.D. in semiotics and had recently returned from a sabbatical in Turin), who had named this domain the Great Forest, a line he had lifted from an important twentieth-century French literary work, Jean de Brunhoff's *The Story of Babar*.

For all his book learning, Dr. Martini was a man who liked to immerse himself in experiences. His new wife—his third I believe, a woman we did not know—was a fellow researcher at his university, and as it turned out she knew a thing or two about wild land and wild food. She had grown up in some remote section of Nebraska and learned to collect buffalo berries from Indians. We decided one afternoon, quite spontaneously, to hike out to a fine section of forest below a rocky outcropping I knew of, have a dinner in the night woods, and then hike back after dark.

With this in mind, we spent the rest of the afternoon preparing pots of rice, chicken, fruit, cheese, and a bottle or two of wine, which we carefully packed in rucksacks. Loaded with our repast, we set out, hiking single file past Charlie's house to a narrow trail leading west from the old road that followed Hurricane Brook. I was, I am sorry to report, thankful that neither Charlie nor Elizabeth appeared to greet our friends that evening. I was afraid our visiting dignitaries might make reference to Spinoza in the course of small talk—something they were given to do on a regular basis. Furthermore, Dr. Martini's manner of dress would have aroused Charlie's suspicions. Charlie feared, above all, the city bureaucrats from the state office who sometimes came to inspect his quarters, and my friend was dressed like a consummate bureaucrat for our outing: street shoes, a white collared shirt, and dark wool trousers. (In point of fact I don't think he owned any other clothes.)

After a mile or so, we came to the site, built a fire, started our rice pot, uncorked the wine, and waited for darkness. The food cooked, we consumed our chicken, and then opened another bottle, cut the apples and cheese, and leaned back on our elbows in the darkening forest, amid the calls of white-throated sparrows, the haunted whisperings of veeries, and later in the evening, in the distance, the yelp of coyotes and the muffled booming of a great horned owl.

"But this is most excellent," Dr. Martini said, leaning back. "It reminds me of 'Le Déjeuner sur l'Herbe.' You women should strip to the waist to complete the picture."

"Wrong again Martin," his wife said sharply. "You're still just a total sexist, and this isn't a nineteenth-century French pastorale. This is wilderness."

I was happy Charlie had not joined us.

With the second bottle of wine consumed, we sat staring into the fire, while little arguments rose and fell between Dr. Martini and his new wife. I was very comfortable and warm with the now quieter chatter of the present company and dozed off. In my half-sleep I heard Dr. Martini suggest that we just spend the rest of the night here.

"Why go back?" he said. "We'd probably get lost anyway and spend the rest of the night wandering around in this godforsaken place, even more lost by dawn."

I woke up enough to agree. It was a very warm night, clear sky, no threat of rain, and so we banked the fire and I fell back asleep.

Sometime later that night I felt quick, sharp scratching on my cheek and woke with a start. Having slept in the open before I knew what had happened. A mouse had run over my face. Awake now, I looked out across the flat section of forest where we had settled. The moon had risen and was illuminating the bold face of the rocky outcropping to our north and had spread a dull, pewter-colored light all through the woodland floor so that all the world stood out like a silverprint photo, all gray and black and filtered, misty distances. Around me were the sleeping forms of my fellow campers, the embers of the fire still glowing.

I lay back and looked up at the leafy basketwork of the tree canopy, and just as I was falling asleep again, from a lake to the west I heard that wild loon clamor that is so much a part of nightlife in the North Woods. I was accustomed to this sound, it had become almost a cliché, but this time it seemed indeed to speak of something out of prehuman time, a lonely wail, the sound of what Thoreau called chaos and old night, or "The Dawn of Man" as Dr. Martini had phrased it when he had heard a loon call a few days earlier.

Having been awakened twice now, I couldn't get back to sleep. Not that I cared; I was enjoying this quiet interlude, and in spite of the fact that we were sleeping on the bare ground, I was comfortable. I lay there listening to the voices of the night woods, the loon call, the rustle of foraging mice, the distant yowl of a coyote, and the occasional hooting of the owls. The moon crossed slowly above the tree canopy, shifting the shadows on the ten-thousand-year-old rock walls to my right. In the shadows, I began imagining shapes—great Titanic Giants out of Thoreau's Chaos, moving dinosaurs, vast human foreheads with shadowed eyes and grim mouths. At one point, out of sheer imagination, an ancient, hunched figure appeared at the top of the outcropping and slowly materialized from the background of trees, sky, and leaves. It peered over the edge, looked down on us, and then, when it perceived that I had seen it, slowly withdrew. My imagination was so fired at this point that it seemed real. This was not by any means my old friend Pan—but some prehuman creature, restored now in this odd, primordial, forested landscape. For one irrational moment I thought that one of the bear-headed men that Charlie claimed inhabited this wilderness had discovered us. With this, everything seemed to fall into a strange perspective. I sensed the horror of prehuman time. I could see the whole world we know as a tiny match snap of human experiment, I could see vast stretches of geologic time, I sensed the emptiness of it all, the meaninglessness of daily life, the spinning planet hurtling across the great arc of the starry night sky through the chill of outer space, and that unfathomable void before the existence of time.

It's no wonder almost all sojourners in the wilderness come, finally, to the question of God.

Oddly, on the heels of this reverie, not fifty yards away, a horrifying, otherworldly shriek shattered the stillness, the caterwaul of a barred owl. It woke everyone up instantly.

". . . the hell was that?" Dr. Martini asked in his thick New York accent.

"Just an owl," I said.

"Jesus Christ, I thought it was the end of time," he said. "What are you? Awake?"

"Just thinking."

"Yeah, me too," he said, and promptly fell back to sleep.

The owl and my people managed to give me some grounding. I lay back again, and, more relaxed now, fell asleep with the benign indifference of the universe.

It was during this same time period—the late 1960s—that researchers discovered lead from automobile exhaust embedded in Arctic ice. I remember thinking after I learned of this that the last place on earth, the only spot free from the effects of human activity, had been thoroughly despoiled now and wilderness no longer existed.

Now the news is even worse: frogs disappearing in remote areas of Amazonia because of apparently unnatural causes, toxic chemicals circulating the globe and raining down on the most pristine wilderness retreats, acid rains killing fish in remote mountain lakes, and immense stretches of primordial tropic lands, supporting as yet unidentified species of plants and animals, as well as known endangered species, under assault at rates of destruction that have never before, in the entire five-billion-year history of the earth, been experienced.

Not long after my sojourn in the Great Forest, I began having unpleasant encounters in seemingly remote sections of the West. Once on a hike in the Aravaipa Canyon in Arizona, I was joined by a perfectly friendly chatterbox hiker who attached himself to me and would have followed me for the rest of the day had I not managed to shake him by a ruse.

On another occasion I got caught by a group of teenagers in what I had presumed to be an empty quarter of the Rio Grande in the Chisos Mountains in West Texas. I had made camp with two wilderness buff friends of mine, pioneers from the American fringes who worked only long enough to finance one trek into the wilds after another—in fact it was from them that I first heard the term "wilderness experience." We made camp on a sandy bank surrounded by high canyon walls where the song of canyon wrens fell around us like rain. It was a beautiful spot to spend the night, but late in the evening we heard shouting and the hollow echo of paddles on aluminum canoe gunnels. Soon a flotilla of four or five high school kids on some wilderness expedition arrived and made camp just upstream. They began setting off firecrackers, and shouting and pounding their canoes like drums—a wild company, free at last from the confines of their zoo cages in the classroom.

The last of these failed expeditions took place on a trail in the Sonoran Desert, where I had been dropped to take a short day walk. I was no more than an hour and a half into the hike, and had stopped to rest by a stream, when I heard a rock fall behind me and turned to see a fellow hiker making his way along the trail on the other side of a canyon I had just come through. My first intuition was to hide; I had a sense of what was to come, but before I could get away he spotted me and waved and made his way directly for me.

He was of a type you sometimes see in the wilderness areas of the American Southwest. He wore tattered jeans, heavy-soled hiking boots, and a purple T-shirt with an image of the Shroud of Turin on it, and he had a long lantern jaw, with a wispy beard and black hair that hung down in rat tails around his shoulders. His most prominent feature, though, was a purple cross tattooed on his forehead.

"Making good time today," he said, sitting down beside me without invitation. "Are you saved brother?"

Uncharacteristically, he pulled a can of beer from his pack, cracked it, and then pulled out another and offered it to me. When I politely turned down the offer he opened it anyway and set it on a rock.

"That's for Elijah, then. 'Case he comes by," he said.

It was about ten in the morning.

"So I come up from the Sabino Canyon the other day," he said without introduction. "Seen some golfers back there, you know, white belts and all, they took the trolley up to the head of the canyon, and so I'm leaving as soon as I see them, I just head out and they say, 'where you going buddy?' real friendly like, but I know what they're after, they're, like, golfers, see? and I say 'none your business,' and so, you know, I'm on my way now—you want another beer?—and then one of them comes at me, like he wants to help me or shake my hand or something and I'm outta there. I don't know where I'm going, but I'm damned if I'm staying back there with all those golfers. But where you going anyway? I'll go with you if you like. What's your name?"

I told him, but I was thinking how to get myself out of this one, so I said I'd better be pushing on, and instead of resuming my hike I started back so I could get away from this madman.

"Where you headed though?" he asked. "I'll go with you, I'm headed your way. Too many golfers back there."

"I've got to get back now," I said.

"Didn't you just come from there?"

"Yeah, but I've got to go back."

"Hey, listen you didn't even ask my name. Don't you want to know my name?"

"Sure, what's your name?"

"Name's David."

"That's good. That's a good name. Well see you later, David," I said, and hoisted my pack and started off purposefully.

"Hey," he shouted after me, "don't you even ask me what David means?"

"David means David, no?"

"No, David does not mean David."

"What's it mean then?"

"Means Son of God."

"Well it's a good name." I was edging away all the while, and he was talking louder and louder.

"You bet it's a good name buster," he called. "Means Son of God, that's what it means. Hey," he said as an afterthought. "You want me to come back with you?"

"No, thanks," I said, "I know the way. But you carry on. And anyway there're all those golfers back there."

"I hate golf," he called out, after a pause.

When I was halfway up the west side of the canyon wall he began calling to me again. I turned and waved and carried on, and he called some more, then got up and followed me. I saw this as my opportunity and when I was out of sight at a bend in the trail I went up into a side gulch, circled around above the trail and, like a mountain lion on its perch, lay down on a flat rock above the trail and watched him pass. Then, at double pace, I resumed my hike.

I remember an old priest I met in Rome some years after this encounter. He was seated on a fallen pillar near the Forum reading his Missal. I saluted him as I passed and he too engaged me in conversation. We chatted briefly, in a civil manner, about ancient Rome, about certain emperors, the good ones, and the bad ones, his family in the mountains, flowers, birds, the weather, America, and all manner of things. But oddly enough, even though he was a man of the cloth, there was not one word of religion.

At one point he said he came here every day to sit on the fallen pillars of the past, beneath the umbrella pines, to read his prayer book and enjoy "the beauties of nature"—such as they were in that busy beehive city.

He seemed anxious to talk, so I asked him if he had had a good life as a priest.

"Oh yes, very good life, but then from where I come, you have not many choices. You grow olives and potatoes, you drive a delivery truck, you leave the village and work in the industries, you go to Germany, or you do as I have done, and you become a priest and you lead a little flock of sheep over the barren hills, and then, as I am doing, you prepare your soul for Heaven."

Then he asked me why I had come to Rome and did I enjoy Italy, and I tried to explain, as best I could, my interest in gardens and my quest to recover that sense of wildness, that spirit of wild nature that I once had known.

"Oh but young man," he said, tapping his chest with his fist. "You are looking in the wrong site. The wildest place on earth, it is here, in the human heart."

I am not sure of the cosmic significance of what followed, but for no apparent reason that I could determine, a bee came winging over my shoulder at that point, flew straight for the priest and unceremoniously, in an entirely irreligious act, stung him on the cheek. He laughed and brushed it away.

"Did it hurt?" I asked.

"No, no, I am used to bee stings. We kept bees at the monastery. I think the bee is an animal with a very long memory. We stole so much of their honey, now word must have gotten around: 'Sting all gentlemen in black robes.'"

"Well, I hope they're done with their revenge for now," I said, and bid him farewell.

Maybe I just have bad luck. Most people don't go out for hikes in the middle of nowhere and meet madmen, or huge packs of noisy teenagers. But I have heard worse stories. I know people who have trekked to remote sections of the White Mountains only to be invaded at night by beer-toting gangs of merrymakers. I am informed that the Appalachian Trail has devolved into a veritable conduit for annoying trail animals who pack along as through-hikers littering and shouting as they go, and I have heard of night camps in seemingly remote sections of parks that are disturbed by the unearthly howls and barks of nearby campers out on a lark.

It may still be possible to get away, and in fact, for many, wilderness is still equated with a version of paradise, a "wilderness paradise" as the phrase has it in so many park brochures. Paul Brooks, one of the old lions of the environmental movement and author of a book on wilderness, appropriately named *Roadless Areas*, felt this way. For him, heaven was somehow associated with wilderness.

Brooks lived in Lincoln, Massachusetts, most of his life, not far from the Italian garden of the Codman estate, and was given to wandering the open lands around his house (much of which had been saved by his own efforts). He died there in his late eighties and was buried in the local churchyard. His funeral, a simple Puritan affair, was attended by many of his devoted followers, both local and national. At one point during the service, one of his friends read a passage from *Roadless Areas* that, as she made clear, may have shed some light on the current whereabouts of Mr. Paul Brooks. It turns out that in this passage he had described his version of heaven. It was not a garden as it was for the Persians, and it was not necessarily a Christian heaven with angels and billowing clouds. It was not even the Paradise of various monotheistic religions, since, ecologist that he was, Brooks allowed for the presence of mosquitoes in his heaven. For him, the afterlife lay at the end of a hard, three-day hike, at a high blue lake surrounded by mountains. Arriving here, bathed in sweat from the long day's hike, you strip off your clothes and dive into the icy waters of the mountain lake. You build a fire and eat fresh trout, brought up from the crystalline waters of the lake, and you watch the serried gold of the alpenglow on the snowy peaks beyond and then sleep the sleep of the righteous on the stony grounds of wilderness.

The thirteenth-century Sufi poet Rumi may have best summed it up: wilderness is a clarity of vision, a wide, silent emptiness where, alone in the world, you experience the peace that passes all understanding.

In wilderness was the unknowable, the emptiness of the Tao, where all questions are either answered or rendered superfluous. Prophets and poets go alone into an unpeopled land, where there are no intrusions, no encroachments of the profane, and no other voices, save perhaps the terrifying voice of God.

Had not the rapacious entrepreneurs of the eighteenth and nineteenth centuries gotten there before the painters and poets, the American wilderness might have offered this same solace. But it was not until the prophetic voices of the mid nineteenth century established the wilderness ideal in North America that anyone in the United States looked upon wilderness as anything other than a threat and an impediment to progress, something that had to be conquered.

Of these voices, except for Henry Thoreau and John Muir, those who first established a public appreciation for the unique quality of the wild America were originally influenced by the worn-out landscape of the Italian peninsula, where humankind had been hunting and cutting timber and pasturing sheep and goats and growing grains for more than two thousand years.

8

The Italian Debt

CLEW: *We can find these enchantments without visiting Como Lake. . . . In every landscape the point of astonishment is the meeting of the sky and the earth, and that is seen from the first hillock as well as from the Alleghenies. The stars at night stoop down over the brownest, homeliest common with all the spiritual magnificence which they shed on the Campagna. . .*

Ralph Waldo Emerson, "Nature"

One of Edith Wharton's favorite playgrounds, the Borghese Gardens in Rome, is now under restoration. Part of this work involves interpretation of some of the original concepts of Renaissance gardens, and I learned from this, and other sources at the Borghese Museum, that some of the earliest garden mazes were created with plant material rather than with stones or turf as in northern climates. According to W. H. Matthews, who wrote one of the first and still the best-researched book on mazes and labyrinths in the 1920s, the Romans often planted border paths of dwarf boxwood in front of their garden porticoes. Pliny makes reference to them in one of his works, and the art of the maze in gardens was rediscovered, or perhaps was never lost, and used again in Renaissance gardens. There was a hedge maze at the Villa d'Este created by four rectangular labyrinths planted with dwarf box, for example.

In the British Isles, the custom of maze building seems to have held on longer than in most areas before it died out. The oldest surviving hedge maze in the world was planted at Hampton Court in 1690 and probably was replanted over an even older maze on the same site. There are others, smaller and not as well known, on estate grounds all around the country. Some of the older turf and stone mazes in both England and Scandinavia were given names, such as the Mizmaze or, more commonly, Troy Townes, a name based on a five-thousand-year-old tradition that holds that the walls of Troy were laid out in a labyrinthine pattern for defensive reasons. The ancient root of the English word "Troy" is related to the Celtic word *Tro*, "to turn," or more closely the Welsh *Troi*, "to turn or revolve."

A labyrinth castle also appears in the Indian epic the *Ramayana*, in which the demon Ravana carries off Sita, the wife of the hero, Rama. Sita is confined in the center of a labyrinthine-walled castle on Lanka and is finally rescued by Rama and his army of apes. They kill Ravana, save Sita, and then circle the ramparts seven times in a stolen chariot at the end of the epic.

There is a similar story in the Old Testament. Joshua had his warriors circle the walls of Jericho, which had all the elements of a labyrinthine urban design, seven times. Then he instructed his seven priests to sound the seven ram's horn trumpets, and then the walls came tumbling down.

Maze lore in general has such ancient, deep roots, and there are so many primal themes associated with this singular design that it is sometimes difficult to know just where the labyrinth story begins and where it will end, which, interestingly enough, is a reflection of the labyrinth pattern itself—a spiraling inward to a center that spirals outward, a beginning without end, a world without end. The labyrinth walker is caught in an astronomical and biological cycle: you swerve to the right with the rising sun, turn, and then spiral left to the setting sun, from birth to death, according to some interpreters, from beginnings to endings, and always inward to the center, to the place of opportunity where, when you have arrived, you spin around, and begin again, renewed.

Mary McCarthy, in her fine accounting of Florentine life *The Stones of Florence*, writes that on first impression there are many similarities between Boston and Florence—a lot of banks, many little shops selling tourist items, and museums full of Raphaels and Botticellis. I do not wish to stretch the point, but there are deeper associations.

For one thing, Florence was, and in some ways still is, the cultural center of Italy. For a while, during the middle of the nineteenth century, Boston was the cultural capital of the United States. More to the point, there is a curious similarity between Florence of the early 1400s and Boston of the early 1900s, or to be more succinct, between the Medici family and the combined families of the Boston Brahmins. Both the Medici and the Brahmins possessed great wealth, and both groups got their money through questionable means. The Medici rose to power in the fifteenth century by cultivating their positions as bankers and tax collectors for the pope, and then wisely invested their gains while leaving a trail of

Medici popes along the way. The Brahmins gained their money through shipping and cotton mills, and by 1900 were able to content themselves by living on their investments. Nothing unique about any of this, except that these two cities were not as involved in military conquests as were other ruling powers. The unique and shared characteristic is that both groups made enlightened use of their money.

Rather than live in vast Medici-like villas or the grand estates along the Hudson and at Newport, the Brahmins contented themselves with smaller, shingle-covered edifices along the New England coast, and with handsome sailing vessels. They put their excess money into libraries, museums, the symphony, land preservation, bird conservation, schools for the blind, and, in what was probably their finest hour, funds for the abolitionist movement.

In Florence, starting with the patriarch Cosimo Medici, the Elder, born in 1389, the Medici family took an active interest in the arts; they funded—so it must seem to the average tourist—half the famous Florentine Renaissance buildings and artworks. Both Cosimo and his grandson Lorenzo the Magnificent (the Medici were not known for modesty) were serious readers of philosophy and contemporary literature, especially Boccaccio and Petrarch. Cosimo the Elder was one of the prime movers of the humanist movement in Italy, part of which envisioned a unity between philosophy, nature, and gardening. He was an avid gardener, and often joined his workers in the vineyard, pruning vines himself and digging in soil. These were readers of Plato, who, according to tradition, established his Academy in a garden. Lorenzo revived the idea and established a school in a garden in Florence for artists. For the Medici, nature, as reflected in their magnificent villa gardens, was a route to happiness, a model of the divine order, which roughly held that God was in his heaven, mankind somewhere below, and below man, nature, but each part related and indivisible from the other.

The essence of the Renaissance garden was nature, albeit a refined nature, selected, arranged, and fabricated into ornaments. Pergolas, trellises, labyrinths, topiaries, grottoes, and waterworks embellished these gardens for over two hundred years. Some evolved into elaborate representations of the natural world. There is a villa above Frascati, the Villa Aldobrandini built in 1598, which once had an ornate "water theatre" as these fountains and cascades and water chains were called. The basic structure of this garden is still in place, although in decline, but when the English architect John Evelyn visited the villa in the early 1600s, it was alive with falling waters and singing birds. The designer had cut into a natural, tree-clad hill and created a cascade that even today falls toward the villa in a water chain, below which is, as Evelyn described it, "a grot wherein are curious rocks, hydraulic organs, and all sorts of singing birds moving and chirping by the force of the water." These mechanical imitations of nature were used also at Tivoli and were employed as jokes or tricks on visitors. Jets of water set in pavement in front of statues where admirers might gather would periodically surge up and drench unsuspecting visitors.

All of these inventions, whether artistic or mechanical, suggested a fundamental view of the natural world, inherently ordered on the one hand, and wild and disordered on the other. Both elements were symbolically represented in the Renaissance garden. This underlying attitude toward nature is one of the connections that binds the unlikely union between the intellectual communities of Boston and Florence. Both groups understood nature as a metaphor for the divine. Renaissance designers attempted to represent this order in the garden, whereas the American transcendentalists of the mid nineteenth century saw the hand of the Creator in the landscape of the American wilderness. The whole process was an evolution; without Florence and the ideas of the humanists and the creation of the Renaissance gardens with their representations of nature as a model of divine order, the idea of conservation or preservation of open space, which had its roots in Boston and Concord in the mid nineteenth century, might never have flourished. The influence was by no means direct, but it was there.

Florentines, of course, never heard of Boston, but the city of Boston was very much associated with Florence. The mastermind of the Gardner Museum collection in Boston, Bernard Berenson, lived at Settinagno, in Florence, and made many of his purchases for Mrs. Gardner there. More importantly, Italy in general, but Florence in particular, had become a literary Mecca for the emerging authors of mid-nineteenth-century Boston and vicinity. In fact, until it was supplanted by the Paris of Hemingway and Fitzgerald, the Italian sojourn was almost de rigueur for worshipful American literary lights, as well as American sculptors and painters.

James Fenimore Cooper spent time in Florence, and so did William Cullen Bryant. Two men of letters, Charles Eliot Norton and William Dean Howells, lived there, and Howells went on to serve as consul to Venice during the Civil War years. Both Henry Wadsworth Longfellow and Nathaniel Hawthorne spent at least part of their lives in Florence, and some of their works have a direct Italian influence. Longfellow did one of the best contemporary English translations of *The Divine Comedy* while he was living in Florence in the Piazza Santa Maria Novella—the old hotel where he lived still has a plaque commemorating his stay. Hawthorne, who spent two years in Italy, lived in Florence before moving on to Rome, where he wrote his novel *The Marble Faun*. Mark Twain rented a villa above Florence not far from I Tatti, where Berenson eventually settled. Henry James was a constant Florentine visitor and set sections of his novels there; he was a grand old ally of Berenson, not to mention Edith Wharton and her peripatetic company of literati. Earlier in the century, the American feminist and educator Margaret Fuller immersed herself in the Italian revolutionary movement, married (perhaps—no one is sure whether they actually ever bothered to marry) the Marquis Giovanni

Ossoli, and died with him in a shipwreck on a return trip to America to raise more money for the cause.

Nothing odd about a young, footloose, lost, new country sending its artists and writers off to look for a voice. What is surprising is the fact that the writers and artists who first led the public to see the American wilderness as a thing of beauty in itself, and not just a hideous wasteland waiting to be conquered and exploited, should have forged this new vision for a New World in the oldest quarter of the Old World.

They were all of them well read in Renaissance studies, and well aware of the Medici influence and the art and literature of the period, far more aware, in fact, than most of the writers and artists of our time. This was especially true in Boston, which by the end of the nineteenth century, in the time of Mrs. Gardner, had become something of an American center for Renaissance studies.

The new American attitudes toward wild land that evolved from the work of these Italian sojourners ranged from the pragmatic, as in the views of the early ecologist George Perkins Marsh, to the spiritual and aesthetic, as with Emerson and the painter Thomas Cole. But as far as the actual conservation of wilderness is concerned, the prime movers under the sway of Italy were Emerson and Marsh.

Marsh, who served as ambassador to the newly united Italian nation, was born in Woodstock, Vermont, in 1801, in a section of the world that, even in his time, had experienced the ill effects of deforestation. The hills around his boyhood farm were stripped of timber, there were log jams in the nearby rivers, flooding was common, and the little topsoil that was left was seriously eroded. Marsh was a brilliant student, too smart and too well read even at age sixteen for the local schools and colleges, including Dartmouth, where he was educated and where he taught for a while. By an early age, he could speak and read four of the Romance languages, and he later learned Scandinavian languages; he knew the classics and was also proficient in mathematics. He was, even as a student, better prepared than some of the Dartmouth professors of his time. After a short stint of teaching, he was elected to the U.S. Congress and was subsequently appointed ambassador to Turkey before being posted to Italy, where he remained for the next twenty-three years, one of the longest serving ambassadors in American history. Marsh and his family lived in Florence, which for a while was the capital of the new nation, and also in Rome. But he was forced to move often since the American government was not forthcoming with salary and he had to find accommodations that he could afford. Toward the end of his years of service he and his family settled in a hotel in Genoa and there, on weekends, he began work on his book *Man and Nature*.

His familiarity with the old, much-lived-in Italian landscape, and the ruination of what was once a fertile land by the Roman Republic, gave him foresight into what the American Republic might expect if it failed to recognize the disastrous course that it had taken regarding the exploitation of resources. Marsh lived in a period when deforestation was the primary, or at least the most evident, effect of human influence on an environment. The extent of this damage in North America appears often in some of the descriptive writings of visitors from abroad, such as Charles Dickens, who wrote an account of the stripped lands between Boston and Lowell in his book *American Notes*. Other accounts by Cole, Thoreau, and the diaries of travelers in the Adirondacks give a sense of the total devastation of a once richly forested continent that had been reduced to barren and eroding landscapes.

Marsh was 63 when he began *Man and Nature*, and he had both the benefit of living in a part of the world that had been civilized for more than two thousand years and the personal experience in Vermont with the effects of deforestation in watersheds. It was clear to him, from his years of observation, that trees in remote hills retained moisture and prevented

---

soil from washing down slopes into streams and, eventually, to rivers. It was obvious that the lack of trees allowed water to run quickly downhill, filling those same streams and rivers and creating major flood damage downstream. It was the sort of information that even a hundred years later, in the early 1960s, had not been fully appreciated by certain government agencies, private timber operators, and land developers.

Marsh documented this abuse of natural land with a short history of the land use of the Mediterranean region for his American readers. He described what he believed to be the almost Edenic environment of the Mediterranean at the time of Rome, the fields of grain, the thick-forested hills and mountains, clear, running streams, and groves of lemons and oranges and olives. Whether this was entirely accurate or not is debatable. More recent evidence suggests that even by the time of Pompeii the wildlands surrounding Rome were so ruined as to have been enshrined as some idyllic past on the walls of the villas. But the end result, no matter when it occurred, was the same.

As its full title implies, *Man and Nature, or Physical Geography as Modified by Human Action* is an account of the effect of the human disregard of the laws of nature—fields washed away, forests decimated, rivers dried to mere intermittent streams. Marsh accurately placed human beings in the landscape as an actual geological force, something that at the time seemed so outrageous that he was labeled a fanatic. Other geologists of the period believed that the world changed only by means of natural geological forces over long periods of time. Although the term did not yet exist, Marsh's views were distinctly ecological. He recognized the interdependence of the myriad forms of life, from the tiny microorganisms to the large, complex species such as wolves and deer. "All nature is linked together by invisible bonds," he wrote.

The book was published in 1864 to limited notice, in fact sales were so low that Marsh gave the copyright to a Civil War philanthropical institution, although allies of his recognized the value of the book and bought the copyright back. Slowly the ideas began to spread. The book was published in London in the same year as the American edition, then an Italian edition came out in 1869, a new American edition was published after Marsh's death in 1874, and another in 1885. The book was recognized— albeit reluctantly—as an important, even visionary work that offered an entirely new perspective on the role of human beings in nature. Until its publication, the attitude, even among the natural historians of the period, was that whatever humans did to or for the environment was beneficial; for example, cultivation was a sign of material progress, a wresting of order out of the ancient chaos.

Man and Nature offered a scientific analysis and a pragmatic accounting of the more philosophical theories of Emerson and Thoreau. Ten years after its publication, the book was influential when activists such as John Muir, who were opposing the destructive land policies of the national government, began lobbying for the establishment of wilderness parks. By the end of the century the idea of setting aside open space in large tracts was an accepted idea, not a radical extreme.

Unlike Marsh, who lived in Italy for a quarter of his life, Emerson was a mere tourist there. But his first journey came at a critical time in his life and had a profound effect on his career. He sailed from Boston in the winter of 1833, in an almost spontaneous manner. He was at a low point in his life. His first wife had died two years earlier, and he was still grieving deeply. Emerson came from a long line of Puritan clergymen, and he himself was an ordained minister, but a few months before he sailed he had had a major break with the established Christian church and had left the ministry. Furthermore, he was sick. Tuberculosis had plagued his family for years, and Ralph Waldo was suffering from its effects that winter. Nevertheless, when he heard about a packet ship sailing for Sicily, he booked passage, even though he was so sick the captain was not sure he would survive the voyage.

The vessel sailed on Christmas day in the teeth of a northeaster, but the sea voyage, although rough in the first two weeks, actually improved his health. By the time he got to Syracuse on Sicily his mind had cleared.

Emerson arrived in February, crossed to Naples, where he spent a few miserable weeks in the rain, and then worked his way northward to Rome and Florence, where he spent the month of May. From Florence he continued north and east, visiting Padua and Bologna and Venice, and then finally Milan in June. He was in Italy a total of five months, which was actually not a prolonged visit for the period; many of the American sojourners in Italy more or less lived there. But, unlike today's lightning tours, Emerson found the time to explore thoroughly those sites he did visit.

What impressed him most about the country was not so much the art but the landscape, and the varied scenery of the peninsula. He was particularly stirred by the gardens at the Villa d'Este, outside Rome, a place that would inspire Edith Wharton some fifty years later. Here, in the old Roman town of Tivoli, the wide flights of steps below the villa terrace drop down to one of the most fantastic water gardens in the world, a magical country of sparkling fountains, curving little paths lined with rivulets and fountains, and water chains that lead on to more fountains and more hidden gardens, more steps of waters and water chains, and a bizarre wall niche with a statue the d'Este family called the mother of nature, Diana of Ephesus, whose myriad breasts spout jets of water. All of this, fountains, statues, and plantings alike, is knitted together in a splendid whole. Emerson wrote that he wished to keep forever in his mind the image of this place, the piazza, the vast prospect, and the silver river beyond the garden, as the fairest image of his whole Italian experience.

Like most of his educated contemporaries, Emerson was well read in the classics. In Italy he was able to experience the places he had read about all his life, the storied landscape of the Roman Empire. And unlike some of the other American visitors, Mark Twain, for example, Emerson was swept up by the power of the culture, the ancient layering of historic buildings, the ebullient people, and the undercurrent of sensuality. Twain thought Titian's "Venus d'Urbino," now in the Uffizi Palace, the vilest painting in all of Europe. There's no record, as far as I know, of what Emerson thought of this reclining, sensual figure with her come hither look, but given the state of mind that was beginning to affect Emerson while he was in Italy, it's possible that he liked it immensely. He was all of 29 when he first went abroad, he was traveling alone, and he was unattached. And here he was in exotic Italy, a stiff Yankee from a family of clergymen of the old Puritan stock. As a New Englander, he was not accustomed to the bravura and the garish visual expression of the Catholic mass—the incense, the chanting lines of friars, the soaring complexity of organ music, images of suffering Madonnas, Christ on the cross, the great swirling marble statuary of Gian Bernini, and all of it bathed in the rich, filtered light of stained glass. This was the antithesis of the clear light of his simple religion.

Nor was he accustomed to opera, to the colors, to the grand strutting of the performers, the bel canto style, the exotic colorful costumes, and the overt displays of sensuality, both on the stage and in the streets. One could not juxtapose two more different spots than nineteenth-century Boston and Naples, or Rome, or even the relatively staid city of Florence. But Emerson had come to Italy with an open mind, and as he traveled northward he became ever more accepting of this new culture, more comfortable with the language and the people and his own place in the swirl of activity in the streets and piazzas.

There is a description in his journals of a mass he attended in Rome, and there is another account of a visit to the Vatican with the pope in attendance. Rather than rail against the incense and the pomp with good old-fashioned Puritan, antipapist ire, he comments on the beautiful surge of color in the robes of the clerics. By the time he got to Florence, he had loosened his attitudes and his worldview considerably. In Italy he experienced, as he wrote in his journals, the "growth of the true self." In short, he found his voice.

After his return from Europe, he published his first major work, the essay "Nature." It was the first American statement of transcendentalism and expressed, in Emersonian style, many of the ideas on the human interrelationship with nature and landscape that had been floating around Europe as a result of the works of Jean-Jacques Rousseau, Friedrich Schelling, and William Wordsworth. But in the unspoiled environment of the American West, Emerson's theory on primitive nature as an expression of the divine could actually be experienced. Unlike Europe, America still had vast tracts of untouched wilderness.

It was in this same period that American painters, who had previously looked to the old masters such as Titian and Tintoretto and Veronese for their instruction, made a similar discovery and began to turn directly to the unspoiled American landscape for subject matter. In the 1830s, along with the writers, American painters were also flocking to Rome to wander the Campagna in search of fresh material. Many of the artists who later documented the wild spaces of the Americas were there, names now generally associated with the Hudson River School or the vast canvasses of the American West—Asher B. Durand, John Kensett, Albert Bierstadt, and the quiet, intensely religious painter Thomas Cole. These energetic youths—most of them were still in their twenties—haunted the Campagna, painting all day and into the twilight hours, marveling at the purple haze above the Alban Hills, the colorful peasants, the shepherds tending their flocks, brightly painted carts filled with wine casks, the large, creaking hay wains, and the old towers and mountain caves and valleys.

Cole spent four years in Italy, first in Rome and then Florence. In Rome he worked in the studio of the famous European landscape painter Claude Lorrain, and spent his days in the field, under the old Roman aqueducts or at the cascades of the Anio River at Tivoli. He sketched the distant Apennine ridges and the wild violet-hued sunsets over the Campagna. As the Italian sojourn had for Emerson, this experience served to sharpen Cole's views of America. He came to the realization that the landscape of America itself offered a rich source of material, and that although there were no dead bones in America, that is to say no storied past, as in Italy, no cultural traditions, at least there were old trees and unspoiled forests. More to the point, the American landscape offered subject matter that had not as yet been painted. "All nature here is new to art," Cole wrote of the American wilderness, "no Tivolis . . . hackneyed and worn by the daily pencils of hundreds [his fellow painters], but primeval forests, virgin lakes and waterfalls."

It was Cole's student Frederick Church who, at least during this period, most embodied the Emersonian ideal of the American environment as an expression of the divine spirit. His landscapes, his vast stormy canvasses, which in the 1850s were all the rage in America, were conceived as an opening through which one confronted reality. His paintings evolved into veritable icons of a new American mythology. Nature was culture — our own version of culture and uniquely American.

This was the 1840s and 1850s, a period characterized by the swift industrialization of the East, the rise of the machine, and the excesses of timber operations just east of the western frontier. But it was also the time in which Downing was retrofitting the open, naturalistic garden designs of Capability Brown to the American garden, and the time of Emerson and

Thoreau. These writers and painters finally alerted the public to the fact that the great unspoiled American wilderness, with all its resources, all its meaning and beauty and its bountiful wildlife, was about to be destroyed.

As Thomas Cole wrote in an essay on American scenery: "In this age, when a meager utilitarianism seems ready to absorb every feeling and sentiment, and what is called improvement, in its march, makes us fear that the bright and tender flowers of the imagination will be crushed beneath its iron tramp, it would be well to cultivate the oasis that yet remains to us."

With this, the groundwork was laid to establish some sort of legal protection for the American landscape.

9

The Cathedral in the Pines

CLEW: *In many places . . . the canyons widen into spacious valleys or parks, diversified like artificial landscape-gardens, with charming groves and meadows, and thickets of blooming bushes, while the lofty, retiring walls, infinitely varied in form and sculpture, are fringed with ferns, flowering-plants of many species, oaks and evergreens, which find anchorage on a thousand narrow steps and benches; while the whole is enlivened and made glorious with rejoicing streams that come dancing and foaming over the sunny brows of the cliffs to join the shining river . . .*

John Muir, *The Mountains of California*

In the spring of 1868 a thirty-year-old Scottish immigrant named John Muir set out on foot to walk from San Francisco one hundred miles eastward through the Diablo Range and the Sierra Nevada to a valley of the Merced River called Yosemite. Muir had come with his family to this country from Scotland in 1849. His father was a strict Presbyterian, a Calvinist spirit, and a tireless farmer, but instead of remaining on the farm, Muir left home in his twenties and continued a habit he had begun in Scotland of wandering in nature. He explored the region around the Great Lakes where he was living, and then in 1867 undertook a thousand-mile walk from Kentucky to the Gulf of Mexico. Following this sojourn he carried on by footpath, horseback, train, and wagon to San Francisco, which he reached just before he turned thirty. No sooner did he arrive than he set out again, this time for the remote valley known as Yosemite.

He spent the summer of 1868 there exploring the mountains, and then began working as a shepherd, a job that allowed him to continue his explorations of the natural world. In November of the following year, he built a cabin in the valley, opposite Yosemite Falls, and here he remained, off and on for almost six years. In 1894 he published his first book, *The Mountains of California,* which was an account of his time spent in the high glacial meadows and the incomparable Sierra terrain, as well as the wildlife and plant life of the region, and most especially the geology of this raw, still forming, mountainous territory that he called "the inventions of God."

This was, at the time, one of the wildest places on earth. Muir describes the meadows of the High Sierras blazing in the gold of composite flowers, the soaring, luminous walls of the mountains with their icy peaks and their evening flush of alpenglow, their thousand dashing waterfalls with drifting spumes of iris-colored spray, and rocks and trees that glowed with a sort of internal radiance. This whole Sierra Nevada range was misnamed, he claimed, it should have been called the Range of Light rather than a name that reflects only its eternal snows, the *nevada.*

Here, among these cracked and snowy peaks, Muir discovered florid, parklike valleys set between mountain walls streaming with waterfalls that cascaded down to the river below. Muir's description of these fertile valleys sounds for all the world like the Garden of Eden, though a wilder, colder version.

In Muir's time, all this was threatened by commercial interests. Timber cutters had already set up mills among the groves of the sacred sequoias, sheep were overgrazing some areas of the Sierras, and watersheds were stripped and beginning to erode.

Although attitudes were changing, the popular spirit of the nineteenth century, and most especially the entrepreneurial spirit of the business world, had yet to absorb, or at least accept, the growing appreciation for wilderness among the writers and painters such as Emerson and Thoreau and Cole and Church. Land and its minerals and its living things were considered, as they still are today, as resources, things to be bought and sold and used. This attitude has prevailed since the dawn of civilization and was ensconced in the Judeo-Christian tradition in that singular biblical command to be fruitful and multiply and have dominion over the earth, and the doctrine would not easily be dug out by the voices and canvasses of a few eccentrics who saw in wild nature the very handiwork of God. But that didn't stop the believers from speaking out, and John Muir, who cited as his primary educational institution the "University of Wilderness," became a prime mover for the cause, a senator-at-large for the outdoors whose platform was to have wilderness areas preserved not for their resources but for their spiritual values.

In the 1870s Muir was not exactly a voice crying in the wilderness. The message had already been heard, to some extent, by politicians and educators. In 1872 President Grant had signed a little-debated and ill-understood bill that set aside a vast two-million-acre reserve in the territory of Wyoming as a public park, for the benefit and enjoyment of the people — the place known now as Yellowstone.

The remoteness of Yellowstone had protected it from the inroads of loggers and cattlemen. Muir proposed a similar nationally owned park for the areas around the Yosemite Valley. The difference was that the resource raiders were already there and quite naturally considered it fair game for exploitation. As with many of these causes—protection for Native Americans, for example—the East was more sympathetic to conservation efforts. The reading public far from the western frontier had been softened to accept the idea of preserving wilderness by the pens of Emerson and company and the canvasses of Moran, Church, Bierstadt, and Cole. It was city-bound easterners who had invented the idea of wilderness, and the eastern press welcomed Muir's accounts of the beauty of the Yosemite Valley. *Century* magazine, the same journal that commissioned Edith Wharton and Maxfield Parrish to write and illustrate a series of articles on Italian villas and their gardens, also published Muir's essays. The magazine was not afraid to print, along with his bountiful nature descriptions, his screeds to have the Yosemite Valley preserved for future generations. The tone of these articles, ranging from poetic, spiritual descriptions to downright vitriol, aroused the public. Interior Secretary John W. Noble took up the cause and eventually, in 1890, one million acres around Yosemite were saved as a "forest reservation."

Encouraged by this, Muir founded an organization, the Sierra Club, to continue the fight. This turned out to be a good move, since even after the bill was passed timber operators fought to maintain a stronghold within the valley so they could continue to cut. Fortunately, the conservationists had in the White House a grand old bully ally, one Teddy Roosevelt.

In the autumn of 1903, in the sequoia forests of Mariposa Grove, John Muir came face to face with a sparky little man in steel-rimmed glasses who happened to be, among other things, president of the United States. Muir and Roosevelt camped together under the trees and then rode horseback up to the overlook at Glacier Point and talked late into the night around the fire. For once, it is said, Roosevelt met his match among great talkers; he was spellbound by the enthusiastic stories of life in the mountains spun out by Muir, and he was especially moved by Muir's passionate outcry against the damage being done in the Sierras by the loggers and the cattlemen in the region. After a long night of talk, the two finally fell asleep and woke up the next morning covered with four inches of snow. Roosevelt loved it. "This has been the grandest day of my life," he is quoted as saying after the encounter. The end result of this night in the forest was a victory in 1905 for the complete protection of the Yosemite Valley.

Muir carried on his conservation battles for the rest of his life, but unfortunately he lost his last fight, a battle to save the Hetch Hetchy Valley from a massive dam. The old biblical prophet, white-bearded, seventy-five years old, and still ranting with religious ferocity, died in 1914.

"They will see what I meant in time," he wrote at the end.

John Muir should be living in our time, we have need of him.

Once, years ago, I made the obligatory grand tour of the American national parks of the West. I was traveling with my brother, who had just been released from a stultifying office job and wanted to see America. Having grown up in the same green garden ruins as I had, and having tasted the adventures of trespass, neither of us was given to undertaking this trip by normal means. We had no intention of sleeping by night in hotels or motels, or for that matter even campgrounds. We traveled light and slept "rough," as the English put it, either beside the road or, more commonly, well off the beaten track. Our custom was to find a likely back-country road, follow it for a while, pack our gear, lock the car, and hike for an hour or so, select a good site, and make camp. We never took trails, we would simply bushwhack through the empty land until we found a good place.

Our main desire was to get beyond the sound of roads, which wasn't hard since we avoided the interstates on this trip and strayed for miles on the old Blue Highways of the 1930s and 1940s. In this manner, day by day we crossed the so-called United States of America, an entity whose internal boundaries we, in those bright days, did not necessarily recognize as meaningful. Die-hard environmentalists that we were, we tended to think of our journey as the crossing of a continent rather than a road trip. We moved through the watersheds of the Monongahela, and the Mississippi, the Des Moines, the Missouri, and the Cimarron. We crossed the Appalachia Range, cut through the Clay Belt to the Great Plains and the desert until we hit the great wall of the Rockies, which we crossed at Tiger Pass, to drop down through the Bitterroots and the Sierra Nevada, to that green and fertile land of coastal California and the beaches of the Pacific. Here, crazed with a sort of dryland madness of having made it across an entire landmass, my brother dashed, fully clothed, into the sea and, feigning insanity, began swimming to Asia.

This trip was hardly a marathon five-day dash across the continent. It took us weeks to get there. We stopped often and sometimes stayed for days at one spot, poking around in the little streambeds and mountain valleys, or stopping in the skeletons of little midwestern towns where old men in straw hats still lined chairs up in front of the local hotels and nodded in the shade. We even worked for a while at a few odd jobs to help finance the trip. This was new territory for me, the first time I had been west of the Mississippi, and furthermore it came on the heels of a two-year sojourn abroad. Everything seemed wildly foreign, even though I was traveling through my native land and meeting daily with fellow Americans. At that stage of my life, they seemed more exotic than illiterate Spanish gypsies. Here were lank cowboys in pointy boots and ten-gallon hats, permed countermaids with cigarette-lined faces who addressed me in affectionate terms, confident bankers in gabardine and string ties, and outdoorsmen in plaid shirts and jeans—all of them wide-eyed and bushy-tailed.

As we drove farther into the West we got into the habit of offering rides to those hitchhikers whom we thought might be interesting. We picked up a pretty blond woman in her twenties in the middle of Iowa one afternoon who said she was headed for Alaska. (I later learned that she made it, without incident.) In the Dakotas, we picked up an old Sioux man who told us long, sad stories of his youth in the missionary schools, and one day, driving the empty spaces of New Mexico in the middle of nowhere, we picked up a modestly dressed man with neatly trimmed hair and a small satchel. He seemed a safe and reasonable fellow, except for the fact that he did not want to use his seat belt, because, as he said, it was too confining and he would rather be comfortable and die than be uncomfortable and not die. This should have served as warning.

It turned out he was recently released—so he said—from prison and was on his way home to somewhere. He was a quiet, tame sort, who claimed he had been locked up for check forgery, and as we drove along he spun out a very long story of a fellow inmate who had recently broken out. This prisoner, who was Mexican (our passenger was decidedly Anglo), used to run around the prison yard every day instead of socializing. As soon as he was turned out for his airing, as they all were between certain hours, he would begin to run hard and continue until the prisoners were rounded up again and sent indoors. The Mexican prisoner told the guards that he was an Indian from northern Mexico and that running was an important part of his religion.

The other thing about the running prisoner was that he would steal pepper. "Guys thought it was because he was Chicano, wanted the spice," our passenger said. "But then he used to fill these stolen plastic bags with water, and shake them up and hit them on the wall, see if they'd break. Then one day he jumps, and we don't see him again."

The escapee, so the story went, took off for the mountains, running, carrying his plastic bags of water and a plastic bag of pepper. Two or three miles clear of the prison, he started to drop pepper piles behind him to "blast out the dogs' noses" as our companion explained. Apparently the man made a clean break. He had not as yet been recaptured.

I did wonder, as we drove along, how it was that this man knew so much about the escapee's habits—the pepper piles, the bags for water, and that sort of thing. I figured it was just one more bit of urban folklore, one of those tall, hopeful tales that must circulate around the gossip columns of prisons. But then it crossed my mind that our passenger was carrying very little, and that, as a released prisoner, he would have at least been given fare to the nearest city and some form of transportation, and that perhaps it was he himself who was the Mexican on the lam.

No matter, we dropped him off at some tiny town and drove on unharmed. But for the rest of the day we talked about this man. My brother thought he made the entire jail story up and was just a short-haired little bureaucrat with a trim mustache and an active imagination. Either way it was a good story, evocative of a sort of universal fantasy of clearing out of normal life and whatever prison you happen to live in.

I had recently been working at the edge of the wild maquis in the interior of the island of Corsica, in a region famous for hiding refugees of one sort or another, no questions asked. It seemed to me that this man was part of the same escapist tradition that was supported by the workaday peasants of the region, the idea of the freedom of wilderness, escape from the monotony that is daily life. You outrun the dogs of conformity; you get yourself to a wild place where you live free in the untrammeled hills to nurse yourself back to sanity. It was this same dream that drove Henry Thoreau to a lonely cabin at Walden Pond and caused him to sleep in the open on mountaintops. It was the same sentiment that gave birth to the National Park System, and the possibility of retreat to the sanctuary of what John Muir called God's first temples.

Our big mistake on this trip was an attempt to visit a few of these temples. My brother insisted that we tour the American national parks, since, after all, we were in the general vicinity. But as we drew nearer, before we got into the official park boundaries, we were nearly undone by the sudden appearance of some of the worst clutter of fast food and ersatz cowboy glitz we had seen in the entire West. We were even more appalled by the urban throng inside the parks. By now we were accustomed to quiet, albeit illegal, campsites where the sister stars of the night desert hung over us like angels and the only sound was the yip of coyotes and the descending obligato of the canyon wrens.

The places where we were directed to camp in the parks were squalid, noisy slums by comparison, with radios and the sound of portable TVs, the night yowlings of babies and drunks, and the daytime bustle of a busy gypsy camp, with bands of happy vacationers armed with their motorized equipment and their fishing gear and their cameras. Wherever we went inside the campground we saw little groups of men standing near machines, and little groups of women standing near cooking places. There were shouting bands of children, and strange three-wheeled vehicles, and at one point—a thing of great interest to me—there was, here in God's first temple, an altercation involving a deranged man and a patient, soft-spoken park ranger. What the fight was about I do not know, but as I was returning from the shower rooms (a place of adventure in itself) I came across them and, curious dog that I am, stopped to watch. The deranged camper had been offended by some regulation and was shouting epithets and waving his arms and stamping the ground and walking around in little circles, while the ranger stood firm, sometimes staring off into the branches of the pines as he tried to find new words to explain to the gentleman why he should not do whatever it was he was not supposed to do. When it became clear that the offended camper was not going to comply—strangely it seemed to me—the ranger left. But I heard later that he had come back with a park guard and the obstinate vacationer had been arrested.

Beyond the confines of the campgrounds, the world was even madder. Great throbbing busloads of gawking tourists disembarked at the appointed scenic overlooks, outfitted with video cameras for eyes, some of which were applied so assiduously that the human beings behind the camera lenses never bothered to look at the actual vistas. Even the trails, usually a respite from the road crowds, were packed with hikers. Before we even got out of the parking lots we were assailed by signs instructing us to stay on the trail, to admire the scenic vistas, to watch out for dangerous bears, not to pick any plant material, not to drink water, not to do this, or to be sure to do that—eternal commands, at every turn.

We might have escaped all this, I suppose, if, in the style of John Muir, we had carried on for another three days and left the trails altogether (something forbidden according to the ubiquitous signs). After some days of hard climbing, we would perhaps have come to that high landscape of broken basalt shafts and the terrible sawteeth of the high Sierras, where the air is so clear it might be the same breathed by angels, were there any up here in this godless, hopeless, broken world, where lost parties in winter camps eat their horses and dogs and, on occasion, one another. But as it was, we unprepared adventurers, without back country permits, had to make do with the common dross of scenic vistas.

At one point during this American pilgrimage we stopped at Mesa Verde, and rather than camp at yet another noisy slum, we hid our car, hiked through the brush, climbed down a cliff onto a narrow ledge, and slept there.

We had a peaceful night. But shortly after dawn I was awakened by a little cascade of pebbles and looked up to see on the wall above me the dread jackboots. I raised my eyes and gazed upon a bulging leather holster containing a mean-looking species of revolver, raised my eyes farther and saw, staring down at me, a blue-eyed National Park Service ranger who wanted to know what in the world we thought we were doing.

I was convinced this was to be our last day in the famous open spaces of the West, if not our last day on earth. We would now be taken to one of those notorious American jails where a heavy-set sheriff with porcine eyes lashes you to a chair and beats you, and worse, keeps you alive for more beatings on local fried food.

Fortunately this particular officer of the law turned out to be a most sympathetic fellow, a school teacher who worked as a ranger during the summer. He explained, gently, that we were supposed to camp only in the designated areas (which of course we knew) and that we would have to push on. He wouldn't even let us prepare him a cup of cowboy coffee. But he did stay with us long enough to tell us a couple of good stories about mountain lions and then, pointing to an opening on the other side of a canyon to the north, told us that archeologists had just uncovered another dwelling site inside a cave.

We moved on that day, and not having learned our lesson ranged farther westward and in time entered into the queen of all national parks, Yosemite. This time I was terrified, not by the authorities but by our fellow campers. On one side of our tent site there was a hirsute group of alpha males covered from head to foot in black leather who spent all their waking hours fiddling with immense throaty motorcycles. On the other side there was a pathological creature who did not, as far as I could tell, sleep the entire night but remained on guard in front of his tent with a lantern, as if to ward off the bears, moose, herds of bison, panthers, Indians, and who knows what other imaginary enemies he had determined were out to get him. In back of us was a group of noisy beer swillers, and in front of us, across the road, there was a huge, happy, essentially harmless family, one of whom had an ear-splitting, whinnying laugh, like a braying donkey, that sounded off at periodic intervals throughout the day and half the night. The next day, surrounded by the towering mountains and more of the now dreaded Scenic Vistas, we got stopped dead in one of the worst traffic jams we had experienced since the George Washington Bridge.

We left Yosemite totally dispirited, vowing never to again enter into another region designated by the brown and white sign with the word "National" associated with it.

Certainly Pan would not be found in such a place.

If you read the earliest descriptions of the landscapes that are now national parks, it is interesting that the first sojourners into these wild regions always seemed to reserve religious language to describe the areas. Thoreau, pantheist that he was, felt that he had accidentally ventured into the realm of the gods on the heights of Katahdin and that he had come too soon into their immortal kingdom. John Muir, the son of a religious fanatic, used Christian terminology to describe Yosemite—the "Creator's first temples" and the "celestial city" of the High Sierras, or the "money changers" of timber thieves and prospectors in the "temple" of the Yosemite Valley. To the nineteenth-century and early-twentieth-century visitors, these wilderness tracts were sacred spots akin to the cathedrals of Europe. The vast canvasses that Bierstadt and Moran and the Western painters brought back from these sites to exhibit in the galleries of New York and Philadelphia were meant to overwhelm viewers with the sublime, the powerful and almost terrifying sense of awe that these rugged, inhuman spaces evoked. The wild forests and high valleys of the wilderness were the American cathedrals. Furthermore, in keeping with Emersonian tradition, they were not the work of corruptible, human guilds, but the constructs of the Creator himself. Here you saw His mighty handiwork in all its glory.

Once, on a quiet day in winter, a day relatively free from the throng of tourists that normally flock there, I was leaving Notre Dame in Paris when I saw a poor American tourist who had just entered the cathedral, presumably for the first time. She was standing in the middle of the great forest of soaring pillars, staring upward into the arching mystery of the branching trusses and clerestories and weeping unabashedly at the splendor of it all.

Never, in all the time that my brother and I spent in the national parks of the West, never in any of the subsequent visits that I have made to the parks, or to national monuments, or to any of the scenic wonders of the Americas, have I ever seen a tourist staring out at a vista, swept to tears by the power of the place. And yet, this spirituality, this pure force of wild nature, the unexpected religiosity of place is why these sites were originally preserved.

The Fate of Earth

CLEW: *The new-comers . . . prospered in this landscape partly because their ground axes could keep back the trees from the clearings, and raise huts above the level of the marsh, but chiefly because they were now independent of the great herds which had vanished into the Northern tundra.*

G. Rachel Levy, *Religious Conceptions of the Stone Age*

In the summer of 1899, Edith Wharton and her husband Teddy were staying high in the Swiss Alps near the Splügen Pass among precise, immaculate gardens with perfectly clipped trees and vines and cooling waterfalls. From her high perch she could see the carriages arriving from Italy and they evoked in her a sharp nostalgia for the smell of incense in old dark churches, for ancient mosaics, vines, overwhelming mulberry trees, campanile, hot plains and cool hills, a mirage of domes and spires and ornate altars. "Was it—ever well to be elsewhere when one might be in Italy?" she wondered.

As a child Wharton used to play on the grounds of villas such as the Doria-Pamphili and the Villa Borghese. Her first novel, *The Valley of Decision*, was set in Italy in the eighteenth century, and she claims that it resulted from her having absorbed in her youth and her later travels so much of the atmosphere she had so long lived in. The immediate result of the publication of this novel was a request for a series of articles from *Century* magazine on the villas of Italy. The stories eventually became the book *Italian Villas and Their Gardens*, which was published in 1904 and illustrated by the painter Maxfield Parrish, who was the height of fashion in America at the time. It was said to be an odd combination. Parrish was a populist magazine illustrator and Wharton a commentator on the elite of the American culture. But the book sold well.

The following year Wharton completed the garden for her American estate, The Mount, which she had planned and built on a 113-acre tract of farmland in Lenox, Massachusetts. She had help with the building designs from Ogden Codman, but the gardens at Lenox were laid out by Edith's niece, Beatrix Farrand, who was one of a group of woman landscape architects who were beginning to emerge during this period.

Quite naturally, with all this grounding in Italian villas and their surrounding environments, Wharton took great care siting the house and the formal gardens at The Mount. She constructed the main house at the top of a meadow to take advantage of existing views and the surrounding terrain, and laid out a tripartite design for the grounds, with the center section of the back of the house as the starting point. From here she designed three descending, grassy plots, bordered, in the Italian style, with evergreen trees, in this case arborvitae and hemlock rather than the traditional cypress, which of course does not grow in New England. Below this, at right angles, she planted an allée of lime trees, with a flower garden on the left and a sunken garden on the right, as viewed from the house. From the terraces and windows of the main building, she could look down across a formal structured ground to a wilder meadow, brushy land with a meandering brook, and, at the base of the hill, a pond backed by a ridge of distant hills.

It was all in keeping with the traditional concepts of Italian villa design—the idea of integrating formality and a built environment with the surrounding natural landscape. You would have thought that this great soul, whose singular enduring interests in life were gardens and books, would have finally come to rest in this place and settled here forever. But there was something missing.

The Mount was Edith Wharton's first real home. It was also a work of art, the only time she put her creative efforts into anything other than her writing (unless you consider the art of friendship). She and her husband, who, incidentally, had family in Groton, just west of Scratch Flat, had moved there in the early years of their marriage after having lived in Newport among the stifling (to Edith, at least) society of the New York rich. Edith was always restless on the coast, and she was constrained by the social mores of this elite group, which, in the main, considered suspect anyone with even a passing interest in arts and ideas. Through friends in Lenox she found the land and set out to build a place in the style of her interest.

Hers was an odd, sexless, fin de siècle sort of marriage, consisting mainly of friendship. The two of them shared an abiding interest in small dogs and spent a great deal of time talking about nothing. Teddy was fond of illness. He was a gentleman and an outdoorsman, a mindless sporting type who never fit in with Edith's ever-widening circle of influential and intellectual friends. Eventually they divorced, but for years their differences were manifested by a certain restlessness; they were always running off to Europe for one reason or another, and they often traveled separately and spent entire seasons apart.

There is another little indication of her general restlessness with the American shores, though. In a line she wrote to a friend in July of 1905, quoted in the Introduction to a 1988 edition of *Italian Villas,* she describes the beauty of the massed flowers in the gardens at The Mount—the lilacs, the crimson stocks, the snapdragons, the penstemons, the hollyhocks of every shade, and the intense blue of her delphiniums. "It looks for a fleeting moment," she wrote, "like a garden in some civilized climate."

There is an obvious suggestion that New England, and by extension, perhaps, America, is *not* a civilized climate. That is a sentiment you encounter again and again in Wharton's nonfiction writings. Like her compatriot and friend Henry James, she was more comfortable in the Old World. She lived at The Mount only five years and even then made frequent visits to Europe. She returned to Italy throughout her life, and then, after she divorced, ended up living in France, where she died in 1937.

There was already a change taking place in the landscape design standards of American gardens in the decades before Wharton published *Italian Villas.* The old picturesque designs, the concepts of Downing, Vaux, and Olmsted, were giving way to the more European ideas of formal gardens. Part of this was due to the fact that rich Americans were importing trained head gardeners from England and Scotland to work on their estates, and these people, who were skilled horticulturists, brought with them their own ideas of what a garden should look like. Architects such as Ogden

Codman shared this interest, and the rich, not having many ideas of their own (save of course for Wharton, who had many ideas of her own and was also rich), went along with what they were told was in fashion.

The renewed interest in Italian villa gardens, although helped along by Wharton and her book, was actually set in motion in the United States by the artist turned landscape architect Charles Platt, who was associated with a group (which included Maxfield Parrish) that lived and worked at the small colony of artists at Cornish, on the New Hampshire side of the Connecticut River.

Platt was one of the original painters in the Cornish colony, but in the 1890s, after having visited Italy during his student years, he began experimenting with landscape design and, in 1892, created a design for his own property at Cornish. In the spring of that same year, he and his brother, who was an apprentice to Olmsted, undertook a trip to Italy to view the extant villa gardens.

Platt stayed for six months and visited some twenty-four different gardens, which he photographed and mounted in albums. Two years later, he published a book called, appropriately, *Italian Gardens,* which included these photographs, accompanied by his own sketches and etchings, and a description of some of the villa gardens in the Roman Campagna and around Florence. *Italian Gardens* began to exert some influence on American gardens and eventually ushered in a decade of similar works on Italian garden design. Part of the popularity of Wharton's book, at least in the beginning, was the presence of the illustrations by Maxfield Parrish. Reviewers praised the illustrations, but had some questions about Edith's almost technical descriptions of the gardens.

At Cornish, Platt had a protégée named Eleanor Biddell Shipman, who picked up on the formalistic elements of the Italian model and began working them into her plans. Other garden designers followed suit, and by the 1920s Italian gardens were almost de rigueur among those who could afford landscape architects. These, of course, were not real Italian gardens; there was an American overlay to them, but the basic concept was there. As Platt and others had pointed out, the Italian word *villa* implies setting as well as structure—the house in its landscape, with its flow of terraces and gardens leading outward into the world of the surrounding lands. The American versions relied on this same principle.

After 1900, women landscape architects such as Shipman and Beatrix Farrand were becoming a force in garden design, and they favored the use of flowers in the more or less formal gardens. This increasing interest in horticulture was not confined to the rich, however. Women had been growing flowers in the dooryards and gardens of America ever since the Downing era. There is, for example, a tiny restored dooryard garden of a typical worker's house of the period in the Seaport Museum at Mystic, Connecticut. And, given the condition of our contemporary cities, there is a nostalgic description of little dooryard gardens in Worcester, Massachusetts, in Carl Jung's memoirs, recounting his sojourn in the United States in the early part of the twentieth century.

Many of these American Italian gardens are still around, in various stages of decline or restoration. There was a particularly evocative one on the heights of the Palisades above the Hudson River in the town in which I grew up, and there were many others, also in decline, scattered around the community, one of which I used to pass every day as I walked to school. I spent all the Saturdays of my childhood stalking the decaying walls of these gardens, hunting frogs in the cracked reflecting pools and dueling imaginary enemies amidst the fallen pillars, vine-covered pergolas, and canted terraces.

Most of the extant or restored Italian gardens are private, but there are a few, such as the Codman estate, now managed by the Society for the Preservation of New England Antiquities, that are open to the public.

One of the regions where these grand gardens are best represented is the east bank of the Hudson River Valley, in the area where Cole and Church and other artists of the Hudson River School lived and worked. The natural scenery of the region provided a variety of visual environments: the wide river, the shores banked with high hills and cliffs, more hills in the distance, and the whole of it, by the 1800s, dotted with the grand estates of the New York families who retreated there.

These estates were small compared to the European villas and chateaus, although one of the last of the European-style feudal holdings, that of the Van Rensselaer family, once encompassed some seven hundred miles all told of Hudson River shoreline. The grand manors were designed with the soft foreground of a smooth lawn close to the house, groupings of trees holding at bay any disturbing views of neighboring estates, and, below the lawns, the river and the sharp ridges of wooded hills on the west bank, which was never developed to the extent of the east bank. The finest estates were located between Hyde Park in the south and the city of Hudson in the north, and many of them are still there today and now open to the public. You can actually see much of the history of American garden design in a single day if you are ambitious.

Wharton penned an idyllic description of one of them—probably the Livingston house—in her 1905 novel *The House of Mirth* that sums up in a very few lines the essence of the Italian garden design. She describes the grounds from the prospect of an upstairs window, the yellowing leaves of the September trees, and the perspective of "hedges and parterres leading by degrees of lessening formality to the free undulations of the park." Beyond that immediate view was the river, beyond that the rising landscape of the wild Catskill Mountains and the hope and the mystery of wilderness.

In 1903, at the height of his career as an illustrator, Parrish sailed to the Italian peninsula to make sketches and photographs to use as subject matter for the illustrations for Wharton's book. He spent three months there with his wife, trying to enjoy the landscape, but there were extraordinarily heavy rains that spring that hampered his travel. Parrish had a style that involved a layering on of many thin coats of paint to create the interior light for which he was best known. He specialized in atmosphere, a flat, yet glowing light that seems to permeate the whole scene rather than emerge from a single source. The generation of the early 1900s practically grew up with his art, since his work was used in a variety of popular magazines, advertisements, and calendars. It used to be said that there was not a middle-class household in all of America that did not at one point have a color plate calendar by Maxfield Parrish.

I always thought these oddly lit landscapes were an invention until I went to the lake district of Italy. At certain times of day, in certain seasons, you see the same luminescent quality of light there that seems to emerge from within the bare, hardened peaks of the mountains that surround the lakes and the blue-green depths of the waters.

I had first come to the lakes district in autumn by train from Switzerland, from Neuchâtel, through the Alps, to the town of Lucarno on Lago Maggiore. In Switzerland the day began as one of those dark, mountain mornings, with low scudding clouds spitting rain and a sharp autumnal chill in the air. The train began to climb and soon we were charging through tunnels and across steep mountain valleys, with the higher peaks lost in gray, snow driving onto the little clustered farmhouses, and plumes of wood smoke billowing from their chimneys. The weather grew worse at each stop, the flakes increased in size and began piling on the roads and the roofs, and then, suddenly, at the end of one of the long, darkened tunnels, the train burst into full sun, and we could see green earth and palm trees at the railroad stations. Ahead lay Italy and the flower-strewn lake isle gardens.

From Lucarno I took the lake steamer down to Stresa, in Italy, stopping at the little lakeside villages along the way, and the next day I went out to the island gardens of Isola Madre. It was there, waiting for the last ferry at the end of the day, that I saw against the mountain walls to the north that odd glowing light, a real-life version of Parrish's pseudoclassical landscapes—the same rocky mountain slopes chiseled by raking light in the foreground, and fading to nothingness in the yellowing backgrounds. I felt I was living in an illustration.

The island gardens of Maggiore, and the gardens at Villa Carlotta and the Villa Melzi on Lake Como, were somewhat later additions in Italian garden history, having been laid out in the seventeenth and eighteenth centuries rather than the quattrocento. These villa gardens have the advantage of some of the most spectacular settings of any gardens anywhere in the world, with the green waters of the lakes surmounted by craggy peaks. There are palm trees associated with some of these gardens and, in season, there is snow on the mountains, and unlike many other spectacular lakes of the civilized world—Lake Tahoe, for example—the shoreline has not as yet been totally destroyed by the clash of modernistic architecture and commercial signs. As one of my friends said when he first saw Bellagio, "this would be a good place to die."

The garden at Villa Carlotta, across the lake from Bellagio, was originally planted as an arboretum and has some ancient and exotic trees. Interestingly enough, some of these "exotics" are quite common on my home territory of Scratch Flat, American beeches, red and black oaks, maples, and larches. Having been planted in the eighteenth century and protected ever since, these are now immense old veterans, the sort of tree that John Muir and the early members of his Sierra Club sought to save from the loggers' ax. On Lake Maggiore, at Isola Madre, and the shiplike, overly built hanging gardens on Isola Bella, you are never far from the lap of water. At every turn of the garden path you are caught in the green walls of ficus, buried in caves of enclosed walls and tunnels of trees and azaleas, and the sunny stucco of the villa walls. The Borromeo family, which has been associated with these island gardens since their inception, often performed little theatricals in an upper chamber family theater in their villa at Isola Madre, and some of the old masks and costumes are still there. I noticed sitting on a back shelf, along with Pulcinella and Columbine and many of the other characters of the Comedia del'Arte, a mask of my old favorite devil, Pan.

Pan may have eschewed the overly controlled baroque gardens of Lago Maggiore, although he might have found some refuge in the little, forgotten corners where the gardeners forgot to clip. However, to see his territory you have but to raise your eyes to the wild scarps across the water and above the ever so civilized lakefront villas with their walled arcades and plantings, to the place where the pastures give way to forests and the forests to rocky screes and unclimbable peaks. Somewhere up there, in a craggy valley where no one goes, or above some forgotten stream, he probably sleeps at night. Parrish himself may have spotted him there. He has a painting of Pan, seated on a flat rock by a rushing cascade, pipes held at his chest, as if in reflection. If you don't find Pan in the high hills look around the gardens some more. He's represented in the statuary and the paintings inside the villas.

On one of these jaunts in the Italian lakes I met a tweedy English lady on the ferry to Bellagio who quite believed in the existence of Pan. I had mentioned that these rocky torn slopes would be a good place for him.

"Oh but there are better places in this world for the Great God Pan," she announced.

She was one of those seasoned English travelers who seem to have been everywhere in the world at one time or another in their lives, and have the ability to take pleasure, or at least endure without complaint, some of the nastiest hardships known to travelers—exotic diseases in western China, an unexpected military coup in West Africa with canceled flights, threats of imprisonment, no lodging, and no food supplies for a week. She had taken the fever on the upper reaches of the Amazon. She had traveled through the Mountains of the Moon in Ethiopia, by herself, during times of political upheaval, and had lived to tell the tale, and she had been to a cliff, somewhere in western China, where your shadow can be cast across a whole forested landscape below the cliff. At certain times of day this shadow is surrounded by a halo of light.

"There are tigers in the forests below that cliff," she told me, "and I was informed that they are the fattest tigers in all of Asia, don't you know. The shadow makers become mesmerized by their giant image and its halo and fall into the jungle below and the waiting jaws."

Her respite from travel was Bellagio. She came every year in late summer, she said, to a little hillside villa and remained till the cold set in, whereupon she would move farther south.

"You never stay home in the garden of England?" I asked (we had been talking about gardens of the world).

"England, my good man, is no longer a garden. It's a squalid little industrialized island where no birds sing. You get word of one little rare sparrow there and all of Britain flocks to see it. How could birds live in England now, with all those roads. I only go there to take care of my mother."

"How old is your mother?" I asked; this woman seemed old enough to be my own grandmother.

"She's getting on I'm afraid. Very frail, although she still gets out to the garden from time to time, one hundred and two, I should say."

I saw this same woman the next day in the gardens of the Villa Melzi in

Bellagio. She was still dressed in her tweeds, sitting on a bench beneath one of the cypress trees near a little lakeside temple, reading. Then I saw her again sitting alone at a café in the evening, from time to time joining a running commentary with a neighboring table of fellow *Inglesi*. These people were very comfortable in their place, and I noticed that, although they murdered the accent—probably on purpose to prove they were English—they all spoke Italian. It turned out they came here every year and knew each other.

They were part of a long tradition. It was the English who discovered Italy as a vacation place, starting in the eighteenth century and early nineteenth century with the Romantic poets. There was such a large colony of English living in Florence by the early 1800s that Shelley referred to the city as a paradise of exiles. There were English schools, English newspapers, eight English churches, and even English doctors. The city was almost an English colony there were so many. By the time of Henry James and Edith Wharton, they were still there, and it is little wonder that so many famous English language novels of the period were set in Italy. Even into the twentieth century Italian culture served as a sort of metaphor for the conflict between the passions of the south (the *supposed* passions of the south, at least) and the cold rationality of the north. It's interesting, though, that this idea is not necessarily reflected in the gardens. In fact the opposite seems to be true.

During the nineteenth century, probably as a result of having so many English around, the so-called *giardino inglesi* became fashionable in Italy and, at least according to Wharton, some of the finest examples of old Renaissance villa gardens were destroyed during this period and replanted in the *Inglesi* style. The original English gardens were influenced by the Italian Renaissance gardens. The new *Inglesi* style in Italy was essentially an adaptation of the parklike designs of Capability Brown, with the pseudonatural landscapes of open swathes of meadow, or *pratos* inter-

---

spersed with clumps of trees. There is a fine example of an English garden beyond the walls of the Villa Petraia near Florence. Originally the landscape around the villa was that of ancient Italy, olive grove and fruit orchards, mixed with pastures. In fact the site was once a medieval castle until it was transformed, in 1537, by Cosimo de Medici and laid out in a contemporary Renaissance style. In the nineteenth century the land beyond the garden wall was transformed once more into the English style, and now the landscape beyond the walls of the villa, which still maintains the old formal Italian designs, has grown up to forest glades interspersed with flowering meadows, the sort of landscape design such as might be found in Central Park or the estates of England, all very un-Italian.

One would think this would be an advancement, something that would have been appreciated by garden lovers, since the English were skilled horticulturists. But in the process of creating these new gardens, the old underlying structure, the balance between formality and disorder, between garden architecture and house architecture and the placement of the whole in the architecture of the land, was destroyed, according to critics. There was, furthermore, a deeper connection in the structure of the traditional Italian garden that was lost, the unstated bond between architecture and the literature and poetry and mythology of Italy, and the design of the villa gardens. The Renaissance garden was a reflection of the culture; they were best understood by association with the enchanted gardens of Tasso, for example, or the spiritual journey of Dante, or the mythologies of Rome and the fables of the poet Ludovico Ariosto. These places were quintessential Italy and to have these English impostors, most of whom didn't even speak the native language, alter these traditions must have seemed anathema to Wharton, who was a great lover of Italian culture. (Never mind, by the way, that the people who made the alterations were, in most cases, the Italian owners of the gardens.)

Edith Wharton laments somewhere that while she was traveling around Italy collecting designs for *Italian Villas*, she would pull up to some known historic villa (she was a great motorist, incidentally, one of the first women to take the motor car seriously) and all she could find were the old buildings with the gardens ripped out, and a lumpy lawn with a circle of flowers and a banana tree in the center. She'd ask the whereabouts of a certain villa or the state of the local gardens and would subsequently be informed that she must be talking about such and such a place, which was still using the "old style" in the villa gardens. What was true in 1903 is even more true today. Some of the finest Renaissance gardens, which were extant even into the 1950s, are now despoiled. Restorations at the Villa Doria-Pamphili in Rome are made in cement, the statuary of many a fine old Roman garden is abused with graffiti, and I have heard that the historic garden of Andrea Doria, in Genoa, is now traversed by a motorway and overrun with feral cats.

There is a restored Renaissance garden at the Villa La Pietra, which is now owned by New York University and is used as a center for Italian studies. The original villa was a spacious mansion built in 1462 and surrounded by an extensive Renaissance garden set in the hilly countryside about a mile north of the city. As with many of the old gardens in Italy, this one was made over any number of times, once in the sixteenth century, and then in the nineteenth century, in the English style, and then again in 1908 for its English owner, Arthur Acton. Arthur's son, Sir Harold, a man known for his aesthetics (and his eccentricities, it should be said), subsequently remade the gardens in their original Renaissance design, although there is, according to garden critics, a great deal of Anglo-American interpretation of what exactly an Italian Renaissance garden was. The basic structure of the old villa remains, however: terraces crisscrossed by hedges of boxwood, narrow strips of grass, and a series of axes and cross axes dropping down from the main terrace behind the villa.

The street outside the Villa La Pietra is one of the routes to Bologna, and is well traveled and populated by speedy little Fiats and, at the other end of the scale, ponderous, stinking local buses, one of which, on a sunny autumn day, dropped me at the great, foreboding villa gates that held the outside world at bay.

Getting into this sanctus sanctorum had taken a bit of trans-Atlantic negotiations on my part, none of which, when I actually came to visit the garden at the appointed hour, had been conveyed to the Italian officials who run the place. I had to talk my way in via intercom.

Once inside the gate the world changed abruptly. Gone were the racing Fiats and lumbering buses and impatient drivers. The great wooden gates closed behind me and ahead, in stillness and calm, lay the classic cypress-lined gravel drive, the trees interspersed with blossoming roses, and fields dropping away to other villas on either side. Since I was alone here, with no one else around, and connected to the grand, closed-up mansion only by the disembodied voice on the intercom, I felt like an intruder, or an explorer in a new country, as I ascended the long drive. I was half hoping to be challenged by someone, a pike-bearing guard in striped stockings and pantaloons, or perhaps by doddering old Lord Acton himself—or at least the ghost of Lord Acton, for he was long gone by the time I was there. But as it was, the grounds were empty, save for one old gardener with a pipe, who winked at me as I passed and carried on with his rake over his shoulder. I spent the whole morning lounging in the sun, poking around the famous Venetian marble statuary, sniffing the rich mold of the old potting sheds on the west side of the property and the baked, dry sunny shed on the east side, and admiring the fine crops of mushrooms that were sprouting through the weedy grasses of the little rooms of the garden—lively, glistening suilius, a healthy stand of shaggy manes, and a mess of edible boletes, which, after some debate, I surreptitiously collected and carried home to my son's apartment to cook for dinner.

Save for a few visits to the gardens at Ravello and Tivoli, this was my first conscious effort really to look at these gardens as an expression of a landscape. I knew enough by this time to admire the integration of the architecture of the place, the breaking sweep of the stairs, the classical use of axes and secondary axes, the privacy of the garden rooms, the old trees, the romance of broken walls and broken statues. Toward the end of the day, as I wandered through these hidden rooms and green allées, the old garden magic of Edith Wharton suddenly descended upon me.

South of the villa, in a more or less uncared for section of the garden, there was a little fence, and beyond that an olive grove, a rough pasture, and the descending sweep of a hill giving on to other villas, other gardens, and groves of olive trees. There was none of the American sublime here, no jagged peaks and terrible, raging rivers with dead bear cubs—this was the quintessential pastoral, the tamed universe. Here was a place for people and nature, and everything fit. It was a humane, integrated placement of buildings and gardens set among surrounding hills.

Beyond the fence, an old gardener on another property was burning trash, someone else nearby was hammering, roosters were crowing all across the hills, the November sun was warm, the smell of earth was heavy. Once more, as if lifted by a rising sea wave out beyond the breakers, I felt a welling of a sense of the place and could imagine this spot as it once was: the smell of boxwood, the weight of ancient history in an ancient land, the flow of the garden rooms from villa to terrace, from terrace to *prato*, and onward and outward to the flowing Tuscan landscape beyond with its pointy cypresses and olive groves and sheep meadows. For all I knew a march of Roman legions might pass, scattering the flocks, or a Renaissance hunting procession might wind through the sharp hills, with its caparisoned horses, dogs straining at their leads, horsemen bearing falcons on their arms, spearmen and crossbowmen, and, at the head of the procession, in yellow and blue silks, his red boots fitted with long golden spurs, Lorenzo the Magnificent himself, upright and proud, and staring directly at me, the intruder from a century yet to come.

Suddenly, in this reverie, I heard a human voice.

"*E bello, questo paessagio.*"

I nearly jumped out of my skin; I thought Lorenzo had caught me trespassing. But it was only the old pipe-smoking gardener passing behind me.

Just outside the gates, I went across the road for a coffee, and here I saw an older gentleman with a small dog, who was equipped with a red harness and apporting a well-tailored plaid winter coat in spite of the fact that the day was warm. I greeted the old man and asked the dog's name.

"His name is Signor Bobolino, and he is a fine dancer."

This said, the old man hoisted the dog by his leash and harness and bounced him up and down on the sidewalk, as he scrambled with all four paws to stay afloat. When he came to earth, he wagged his entire body and in one surprising leap sprang into his master's arms and licked his face.

"Once I thought to take him to the circus," the old man said, "he is so talented. But I would miss him; as you can see, he is my loyal companion, we walk here every day."

I calculated that this man was perhaps old enough to have known Lord Acton himself. I asked as much.

He nodded his head from side to side in a noncommittal way, indicating that he had known him, but not well. We chatted on for a while about the gardens and Lord Acton's restoration, and then the old man took my arm and drew me toward the wall of the little café.

"You know, of course, but perhaps not, since you are not from these parts, that this Englishman, this Signor Acton," he cleared his throat and lowered his voice, "he was not a man who was attracted to women."

He looked me in the eye and nodded gravely, and I nodded gravely in return, and said I had heard this fact, but that I did not spend much time thinking about it.

"That is well. It is not a good thing to think about. Our times are crooked and the way is lost."

"Save for Bobolino here," I said, trying to change the subject, "he leads a good life, not true?"

"O yes, Bobolino has fathered many a powerful dog. He is a captain among dogs."

Bobolino did not look anything like a captain, and given his size I do not believe that he could have fathered anything larger than a Chihuahua, but I let that go too and said goodbye and walked down to Florence on a series of winding back roads. I found a dead weasel on my way down the hill, and one hundred yards farther along, I was stopped in my tracks by the honey-smooth sound of someone practicing on a viola da gamba inside one of the houses. I stood transfixed, and for some reason started thinking about Edith Wharton's statement that The Mount was *almost* a civilized place.

Earlier that same autumn on a quiet afternoon in October, when the chestnuts were ripe in the forested hills of Lombardy, and the little gangs of mushrooms were springing up on the forest floor, my betrothed and I had taken a little walk into the hills to the north and west of the town of Stresa. This, like the national parks and public lands of the American West, must be one of the most tourist-ridden sections of the world. Foreign visitors have been coming to the shores of the Italian lakes in both summer and winter ever since the Roman Republic, and yet the vacation villas and the little lakeside towns, compared to some other parts of the world, have adapted well—more or less. There are no glaring commercial strips such as you would find in American resort towns, and few of the noisy lines of outdoor cafés, discos, and bistros such as you might find in coastal sections in Italy, France, or the east coast of Spain.

We deliberately struck out inland, away from the towns, and walked up a narrow little road to take a trail that a man in the village had told me about. Here the road was lined with high chestnut trees and a few larger houses set back at the end of long, leaf-strewn gravel drives. A half an hour into this walk we still had not come to the little side trail and I began to wonder whether we had missed it.

Ahead we could see an old man with a cane moving toward us step by step. He was dressed for his constitutional in a black suit with a white shirt, and a black fedora tipped rakishly over his right eye. We greeted him and asked if he knew of such a trail. He saluted us, admirably, and then rather than answer immediately, asked what part of Italy we were from. This was mere politesse, I believe; he must have known we were foreign. Then when he learned that we were from America he wanted to know what it was like there, were there many cowboys, was there a lot of shooting, as he had heard, and was it indeed possible to make a great deal of money there without working. We explained that there was indeed, in certain areas, a kind of local who imagined himself a cowboy, but that most of them drove trucks. And we said that there was some shooting in certain sections of certain cities and that, yes, it was possible to make a great deal of money there, but in order to do that you had to apply yourself to the task with a great deal of vigor.

"As always," he replied, with a tip of his head. "And you yourselves?" he asked. "You are enjoying the Italian countryside?"

"Very much," we answered, "very beautiful here."

"And you enjoy the mountain views?"

"Yes," we said. "We have very much enjoyed the beauty of the mountains."

"And you have walked in the island gardens of the Borromeo family?"

"Yes," we answered. "Several times we have walked in these gardens."

"They were a great family in these parts, the Borromeos, very powerful, very generous. I myself am friends with the last of the counts. He lives alone on Isola Madre, nursing his memories."

I'm not sure this was true, but we had passed a small path there a day or two earlier and met a gardener who told us not to enter. "The count wishes to be alone," he had said.

"This count was your friend?" I asked.

"Everyone is my friend. When you get to be my age, and you live in the same place for as long as I have, you know everyone, for better or worse."

"Well it is a good place to spend a life."

"Yes. But, as you will no doubt have to learn someday, it is easier to cross a field than to live one's life." He snapped his heels. "And now signori," he said, "I bid you farewell."

He bowed and kissed my betrothed's hand and never told us how to get to the trail.

We watched him shuffle forward deliberately through the leaves, and then we saw him turn and walk up one of the long gravel drives toward one of the villas.

For our part, impoverished American refugees that we were, we carried on by foot, and eventually came to a narrow path that led up into the foothills. Whether it was the right one or not we followed it, and walked up through thickets of chestnuts, passing two or three steep ravines on either side, all overgrown and mysterious. Higher up we came to a stony pasture where a donkey was grazing. He looked up at us as we came into his clearing, and watched us carefully as we passed, as if he too knew that we were foreigners. In the declining light we tracked upward, and although we climbed for more than an hour through high pastures, we never got to the peak, so we turned and descended in order to get back before dark.

Just before we dropped back into the thick forests, we sat for a while and stared out across the evocative landscape of the lakes region. The light was fading faster now and the lake had assumed a black absence of color, with darker shadows on the shorelines, and the pale yellow and red tile roofs of the lakeside villas glowed with that internal Parrish luminosity. Higher, in the foothills, there was a rich purple hue, and above that the last light of autumn was illuminating the high peaks and the clouds above them so that the two seemed to merge. It all appeared remote, and impossibly wild up there, as if it were indeed the realm of unknowable gods.

Here was an area lived in by human beings for over forty thousand years, and although no doubt sadly altered from the time of the Neolithic, when the first human beings moved into this region and set up their permanent dwellings in lakeside villages on stilts, there was still a feeling of wildness, if not wilderness. Staring out over this sublime landscape it occurred to me that I had been in such environments before. This was in fact what must have somehow established itself as the model for what is meant by the word landscape—not wilderness, by any means, not a long, unhoused, uncultivated tract of unbroken forest or desert, and not urban certainly, but a combination of wild land, pasture land, and villages. It all seemed familiar to me. I thought it was perhaps because this is in fact the landscape you often see in art, the background for the Renaissance paintings of the Flight to Egypt, for example, or the Journey of the Magi, or landscapes of streams, lakes, and mountain roads of eighteenth-century painters, or even the tamed, humane environments of the paintings of the American Impressionists.

Save in summer, when tourists flock through the area, the landscape here has endured ever since agriculture began in this region, sometime in the late Neolithic. In fact, the region is one of the oldest settled parts of the Western world, having sheltered both Neanderthals and Cro-Magnons for over sixty thousand years. I have been to similar spots in southeast China, the Pyrenees, the Yorkshire Dales, and the valley of the Dordogne, and there must be other sites elsewhere in the world where, either because of legal protections, as in the south of France, or by accidents of history or economy, a balance has been achieved. The land endures, the inhabitants endure.

If this were to be the fate of the earth, things could be worse.

II

Backyard Serengeti

CLEW: *The presumption was that the wilderness was out there, somewhere, in the western heart of America, awaiting discovery, and that it would be the antidote for the poisons of industrial society. But of course the healing wilderness was as much the product of culture's craving and culture's framing as any other imagined garden.*

Simon Schama, *Landscape and Memory*

Traditional Christian labyrinths, such as the maze at Ravenna, had eleven courses, with the twelfth at the center, symbolic of the twelve seasons. Some had only seven rings, a reflection of the courses of the seven astrological planets, or the seven days of the week. Mazes marked pilgrimage and redemption; they stood for protection and for secrecy; they were dance floors; they were used as magical, symbolic designs in Hindu Tantric tradition; they reflected the weaving, spinning image of Ariadne in the classical tradition, and the life-giving, woven patterns of the Native American Spider Woman, the Creator. It is hardly surprising that such a deeply engrained image should have been, finally, rediscovered by contemporary artists.

In the 1960s, artists such as Tony Smith and Patricia Johanson began using labyrinth images in their works. Smith made a formal labyrinth sculpture and an outdoor water maze. Johanson began using maze patterns in her organic earth designs, and more recently artists such as Marty Cain have begun laying out healing mazes in feather and stone. Charles Simonds created a miniature maze in clay, and Dennis Oppenheim, in Wisconsin, created a huge field maze of hay bales that was essentially an enlargement of a laboratory rat maze. He then herded cattle through it to encourage them to consume his creation.

After a few years my own maze began to form a structure of its own in my garden. After much tying and pleaching, the two trees on either side of the entrance took on the form of an arch, and the hedge wall on the outside of the labyrinth grew in thickly so that from the house visitors would see a large circular hedge with an arch in the middle, and those unfamiliar with the property might not know exactly what the arch led to and might venture in. My hope was to teach the dog to run the maze by tossing his ball into the goal, over the hedge walls, and then have him run the maze to retrieve it, but this ultimate maze trick never worked. I could land the ball in the center easily enough, but the dog would simply burrow through the lower tangle of branches to get to the goal and then charge back out by the same route, ball in mouth.

There were still many empty places in my pseudo-Italian garden. Once planted, the garden on the southern side of the house rolled out to a black wall of woods and simply stopped. My allée of tall hedges went nowhere. The two narrow garden beds I had laid out inside the hedges proceeded to nothingness, save an old, poorly built, and ill-maintained stone wall, a tangle of dead limbs beyond, and woods beyond that. There was nothing to hold the eye, so that when you looked along the narrow line of the tall hedges you felt incomplete. For a while, I thought one answer to the problem would be to follow a Japanese garden tradition and create a borrowed view, as it was called, in other words, cut a swathe through the forest on the other side of the wall and then take out some of the stones in the wall to let the eye escape, thus creating a long, narrow opening that advanced into the darkness and mystery of the summer woods. That would have been a fine plan, but I did not own the trees on the other side of the wall and there was no guarantee that having done this, the owner of the property, a certain Mr. Smith, known for his propensity to build houses around the town, might not get the idea that this would make a good house lot and then totally destroy my vista.

What I needed was a focal point, something at the end of the allée of tall hedges to let the eye come to a stop, something to look at. The best solution, I thought, would be yet another structure for the property, a small folly perhaps, in the style of Capability Brown, or perhaps a summer house or tea house to retreat to on hot afternoons. The only problem was money; follies of this sort do not come without expenditure.

During this period my paramour and I had been living together for some five or six years in our Andrew Jackson Downing cottage-villa, a social arrangement that, we both agreed, would have offended deeply the moral code of Mr. Downing. For this reason—and a few others—we decided, finally, to marry. One of the results of this happy union was a tea house, the wedding gift of a generous new mother-in-law. My brother, who fancies himself a designer of outbuildings and garden houses, worked out the plans for the building. We decided on a modest, relatively plain structure, along Federalist lines, with an average pitch to the roof, a bird-house hole in the facade under the eaves, and open screened walls. For the front, I finally found a use for two front doors off an old Georgian-style building that was being renovated and modernized. These tall, seven-and-a-half-foot doors were too big even for the tall style of my cottage, which by this time had been anointed "the Vicarage" by my brother, who appreciated the absurdity of my grand plans. I used the doors on the front of the tea house as walls, and screened the arched windows.

The little house sat at the end of a series of garden statements, a circular herb garden, with a bird bath whose column was decorated by dancing nymphs in diaphanous gowns. On one side of the column there was another carved figure, a horrid thing with beady eyes, goat horns, high cheekbones, and a pointy little beard—an image of my personal god. There was a weedy *prato*, in the Italian style, just behind this circular bed, two more elongated herb beds, and in front of the tea house two more semicircular beds of irises enclosing a small, smooth-shaven circular lawn, with the whole of it held in by my double row of tall clipped hedges.

To celebrate the completion of this part of the garden, as well as our wedding, on a midsummer night that year we held a masque. People came properly attired for this event, some disguised as kings or fairy queens, some as warrior princes, complete with doublets and stockings, some as wolves, or bears, or Indian queens, as well as a foreign contingent consisting of Spanish grandees, Italian contadinas, and, of course, the members of the masque itself.

We chose to play sections of *A Midsummer Night's Dream* for the festivity. I played Theseus, the duke of Athens, and my bride was Hippolyta, the queen of the Amazons. We had a contingent of fairies, played by the young daughters of our various families and friends. Oberon and Queen

Titania were in attendance and the "rude mechanical" known as Bottom lounged beside the action in his donkey head, and the whole thing went off without a hitch, save that the Jack Russell, properly fitted out with a mane for the occasion, burst in at the wrong cue, his costume awry, and did not play at all well his appointed role of Lion.

After the performance, quite spontaneously, the players and masquers held a marriage procession, and, also without direction or planning, this company of celebrants, led by Oberon and Queen Titania, made its way through the maze. I looked back at one point and watched this weaving snake of humanity, meandering in its mazy way through the courses, some marchers bowing and dipping as they walked, some strutting regally, and a few immodest ballerinas (most of my friends are middle-aged) pirouetting and executing grandes jettées.

It was not until some years later that I learned that after he slew the Minotaur, Theseus led the liberated Athenian youths out of the labyrinth at Knossos in a similar weaving dance known as the Geranos or Crane Dance. This serpentine dance form became a part of a folkloric maze-dance tradition on the island of Delos, where Theseus had stopped on his way home. Performers wore animal masks and circled round an altar decorated with horns in memory of the slain Minotaur.

Maze dances such as this probably predated Theseus and were an important part of folkloric and religious traditions throughout the world; some of them survived even into the twentieth century in England. Now, with the renewed interest in labyrinths, they are being revived. The dances were performed in the spiraling maze pattern and the dancers followed a course cut into the ground. Originally these may have been based on patterns laid out with stones or pebbles, but in England and Scandinavia, where they were common, they were cut into the earth and were known as turf mazes. There were once hundreds of turf mazes in England. There is even a reference to them in *A Midsummer Night's Dream*: Titania, commenting on the fact that things seem to be going awry, complains that "the nine men's Morris is fill'd up with mud: And the quaint mazes in the wanton green, For lack of tread are undistinguishable."

Now, only eight of these ancient maze sites remain intact in all of England.

Four or five years after I planted my labyrinth I began to accumulate more information on these various maze traditions, and I became especially interested in the labyrinth as a symbolic defense of a place, since at this time I found my own horizons shrinking as the world beyond my garden began to change.

Whereas in the past I used to range out over the wider world of Scratch Flat, poking my nose into every little corner and digging out more history of the place than anyone would care to know, the world of Scratch Flat began to change and my old haunts began to feel more cramped. Traffic increased on the road. Huge dump trucks lumbered by daily, carrying whole plots of earth from one place to another for the veritable assault of building that seemed to be going on in the town just to the north of the garden, where dark armies of developers began laying waste to the ancient civilizations of nature.

In the face of this, I determined to cultivate my garden even more than I had been. I found myself using the garden more and more as a walking place. I wanted to invent there a nation to defend myself from the outside world, and so, thinking to increase my walking grounds, I began designing winding paths all through the garden, a sort of unicursal, randomly patterned mizmaze that took up the whole acre or so and had various side loops that wandered off into grounds not strictly mine, the woods to the west, the lands of my ex-wife to the east, the overgrown old field to the north, and then back onto my land. All of these paths converged, flowed inward toward the entrance to the circular maze, and then wound ever deeper, circling and splitting and turning and spiraling toward that singular, magical space, the ineffable center, the so-called goal, where according to tradition anything could happen.

The often-quoted advice in *Candide,* to cultivate your own garden, is actually delivered in reaction to all the calamitous events that Candide and his optimistic old fool of a tutor, Dr. Pangloss, had experienced. Candide and company, after many adventures and many losses, had ended up on a small property near Constantinople. Here they met an old Turkish gardener who lived quite well on his small holding, albeit surrounded by political chaos. He invited them to share his oranges and lemons, boiled cream and mocha coffee, all of which came from his own grounds. The old gardener knew nothing of local politics, nor the outside world, and yet lived happily. Pangloss and Candide returned to their land, taking him as their model, determined, finally, to settle there and grow their crops. Man was put in the Garden of Eden, Pangloss claimed, to work the land.

This idea of staying put, of digging in in the face of a world in chaos, suited my little garden projects quite well. Furthermore, the idea of the garden as a sanctuary, a place to begin, an Eden, still has meaning in our time, although for different reasons. We don't have to offset the unhoused *deserta* any more, the chaos of wilderness; we need to rediscover it. But the metaphor still works. The garden is not the end, it is the beginning, the place where you preserve the wild spirit that will save the world—In gardens is the preservation of the world, to paraphrase Saint Henry.

In the meantime, while I was at home cultivating my garden and the world was, as I believed, falling apart, others in the community were taking up arms against developers, and in some cases saving land long before the developers even had a chance to bid. One such case was a prime piece of property at the eastern edge of Scratch Flat, an exquisite, haunting (and haunted, it was said) tract of land with an apple orchard that once was the site of a village of Christianized Indians, and was in fact the first settled and cultivated area in the town. The property was owned by a famous old curmudgeon who would not suffer fools, developers, and anyone else he didn't like to venture onto his sacred grounds, but who protected his environment with a passionate intensity. When he died, his executors (as his will urged) did everything possible to save the land from development. The property was offered first to the town, which only a few years before had spent a great deal of money salvaging a tract just west of the land in question. The cost of the orchard was two and a half million dollars, which, given the economies of the time, was below market value. The town officials were anxious to preserve the site, but they had to gain approval through a town meeting. Said meeting was subsequently called, and the great hall, as is usually the case in big, expensive, controversial land purchases, was crowded with people. The current town officials, who do not count themselves among those impassioned political speakers of the past, plodded on in their way, describing the property, and then called for debate. As the local press pointed out after the meeting, debate was the wrong word; the event was more of a pep rally. The vote in the end was overwhelming: five hundred and forty-three in favor of the purchase, seven opposed.

Elsewhere, closer to home, as older farmers around my garden died off or gave up and sold their land, allowing developers to move in, small local groups organized to hold them at bay and save what they could save. There is hardly a town in the region without at least one land trust, which

attempts to buy open space outright. Whenever the fight gets serious
these groups will be backed by regional organizations, and when the land
in question is considered to be of prime ecological value, these will be
backed in their turn by state and national organizations, and in some cases
by nationally known figures.

Such was the case with two proposed developments near Walden Pond.
The fight to preserve the land was fought locally at first, against powerful
developers and one international financial magnate, to no avail. But word
of the impending destruction got out, and unlikely knights charged in
wielding the greatest, and sometimes the only, sword that is feared by land
speculators—money. In this case the unlikely hero was the rock singer
Don Henley, a Thoreau reader since high school, who financed outright
the salvation of the land and then set up an organization to continue the
work and find a home for the then homeless Thoreau Society, a group of
scholars devoted to the study of Thoreauvia. Their finest hour (after the
salvation of the land, of course) was the opening of a great mansion on a
hill, a structure that critics of the group claim would have caused Saint
Henry to cast his most barbed spears. Criticism notwithstanding, the
doors opened and on the dedication day a whole flock of formerly unrec-
ognized and in fact unlikely Thoreau appreciators appeared from the
woods to sing paeans to this American hero. These included no less than a
scandal-ridden president of the United States, his wife, their minions,
Senator Ted Kennedy, whose mother used to take him to Walden Pond
for picnics, and various and sundry local senators, representatives, and
celebrities, including Mr. Henley himself, who started the whole thing.
Graciously, it seemed to me, he kept a low and modest profile during the
ceremonies. The true scholars, those who really knew their stuff, and
those who worked hardest to protect the land, also stayed in the background. This was the hour of the celebrities.

But it was not the well-publicized victories that mattered. It was the little ones, the fifty-acre tract here, the hundred-acre tract there, tiny increments of saved land. If the pattern were to continue and the fashion of putting aside open space to endure, all of these little islands could theoretically be bound together in a series of green corridors to allow the free passage of the wildlife that had so successfully returned to the region with the return of the great forest.

The Great Forest itself, where I had once lived, had experienced such a regreening. It had formerly been extensively cleared, cultivated, and lived upon. In fact the town in which the Great Forest was located had been losing population since 1798, when the few farms that were in the area were first deserted. It struck me that if I could live long enough, the same might hold true for Scratch Flat. The world economies would crash, undone by a lack of resources, development would slow, then halt, and all the little preserved islands around the region with their well of native species would soon overspread the land and the wilderness would be reborn.

Like many sojourners in the country I kept a journal in the time that I lived in the Great Forest. I had started the journal toward the end of my first year, as spring approached, and reading it over even after a long absence I noticed that it still evoked a sense of what it is like to experience spring in a northern forest after having survived the cage of winter. There were steely days of cold, and long walks in the snowy forest, where the mouse tracks stitched the trunks of the trees together and the dry oak leaves hung like sleeping bats. Chill days were followed by a warming trend, followed in turn by nights of bitter cold, and then, finally, a general slipping toward spring. I noted the mating songs of birds in the middle of snowstorms, the arrival of early migrants, the slow sinking of the knee-deep snows, the loosening of the brooks, the thunder of breaking ice, scudding clouds, flights of migrants, more snow, churnings under the rivers, the crack of ice storms, followed by blinding sunny mornings when the whole world was like shattered glass and a walk in the woods in late morning was like walking through a rain of falling crystal.

And then finally, on April first, a long warm rain: the emergence of the very earth from beneath this glacier of a season, and arbutus blooming on the forest floor, and the coral hue of the alder buds, and the red of the osiers, and greening rosettes hugging the moist earth, the night march of spotted salamanders, the bursting, bubbling song of the finches, more rain, mists in the hollows, and then, after what seemed a century of still nights, the call of frogs. And then eggs everywhere, in gelatinous, balled clusters in ponds, individually in vernal pools, ropes of toad eggs, little luminescent dots in swampy streams among newly greened shoots, and the muffled drum in the forest of ruffed grouse, and the piping of war-blers, the mouse ears of leaves, the forest floors strewn with bloodroot and trillium and trout lily, and the unseen explosion of roots bursting forth after a winterdeath, the rising of saps, and the sudden lacework of the leaves of May. And every year like this, every decade, every century and millennium for ten thousand years, and most of this—one could even say all of it—unobserved by those unfortunates who live locked away from daily contact with the natural world.

Down in the hollow where Charlie and his extended family lived, Ansara and C and Zeus stripped off their clothes and ran naked through the woods, their white flesh contrasting with the browns and the new flush of green. And Elizabeth baked another pound cake, and Charlie made another pot of percolated coffee, hauled his last loads of wood from the forest, and once or twice sat down on a heavy plank on the south side of his house and put his old grizzled face up to the sun.

You had to have lived through a winter in that place to really understand spring.

A year and a half after I wrote that journal, I was on my way to the stream to swim and saw Charlie standing in the weeds with an ax in one hand and his other hand on his hip, looking back at his kitchen door, sadly.

He turned when he saw me, but was uncharacteristically silent.

I asked if something was wrong.

"We got the notice today," he said. "We got to leave this here place, forever."

"What notice?" I wanted to know.

"State boys evicting us. We knew it was coming some day, we just didn't know it would be today."

Charlie's house, like mine, was owned by the state department of forestry and we lived there for very little money. My rent was something like seventy dollars a month, and Charlie may have gotten his place for free for all I know. But there was, as Charlie explained, a new program afoot to cut budgets, and part of the plan was to move all the workers out of the state-owned houses in the forest lands. At least that was the story he was told. His "executioner," as he called the little bureaucrat who delivered this coup de grace, was never entirely straightforward about any of this, according to Charlie. The state bureaucrat's logic was that the house was in violation of some new health code and was not safe for a family and was not worth fixing up.

"What the hell does he care?" Charlie asked rhetorically, "we're the ones who're going to die from whatever it is they think we're going to die from if we keep on living here."

Within the month, Charlie, Elizabeth, Ansara, C, and Zeus moved on, taking the dogs with them. I later heard that Charlie and his family were living in a town, no doubt in some boring, better-maintained place with clean floors and a working bathroom. Ansara and C lived somewhere nearby, in another cabin.

A few weeks after they all left, I went into the house through an open back door and wandered around looking at the rooms, the low, sagging plaster ceilings, the narrow hardwood stairs, the fine moldings over the fireplace, and the detailing on the old wall paneling. Charlie and Elizabeth had cleared out most of their things, but here and there I found remnants of a past life—stuffed bears belonging to Zeus, some old machine parts in the kitchen, a kerosene can, a hairbrush discarded by Ansara, who rarely combed her hair anyway, one of Zeus's coloring books, marked, I noticed, with outrageous oranges and purples and with absolutely no reference to the outlines of the bears, lions, and princes therein. Upstairs, in what was once their bedroom, Elizabeth had scrawled a message on a wall with a red crayon. "This was our home for twenty-two years and we raised five children here. Signed Elizabeth J Parsons."

One sad afternoon I was driving down the hill road west of the town and saw across the valley a column of smoke rising from the woods, in the vicinity of my house. I hurried along and found an array of red fire trucks on the north side of the road surrounding Charlie's place. The local firemen, some of whom were part of the forest service and more used to fighting forest fires, put up a brave defense, but the fire had been burning for a while before they got there and there was nothing much they could do except keep the flames from spreading to the nearby woods. They had doused the weedy clearing surrounding the house, as well as the trees, and slowly, over the course of two or three hours, the fine old eighteenth-century house, with its mullioned windows and its center chimney, consumed itself and fell into its own cellar hole. Within the week, after the cleanup, it was just one more old house foundation that dot the forests of the north. Dead without a history.

Through the post office grapevine I heard Charlie's opinion on the matter, which was that the state had had some hand in the fire. "It was, how shall I say, a very 'convenient' fire," someone in the post office pointed out.

Less than six months later, a state official called me and informed me in a slightly nervous voice that I too was to be evicted as part of the same program that undid Charlie.

In a reversal of the old Biblical story, I had been thrown out of the wilderness.

The Persistence of Pan

Be still O green cliffs of the Dryads
Still O springs bubbling from the rock
and be still
Manyvoiced cry of the ewes:
It is Pan
Pan with his tender pipe:
the clever lips run
Over the withied reeds
while all about him
Rise up from the ground to dance with joyous tread
The Nymphs of the Water
Nymphs of the oaken forest

Plato

After twelve turns, after a symbolic pilgrimage, after winding to and fro among the green leaves of summer, the yellow leaves of autumn, the spare, brushy twigs of winter, and the pearly little green pea buds of spring, you will come, eventually, to the goal, to the very heart of the maze, the place where, according to legend, anything can happen. Here, in effect, is the omphalos, the navel of the world, the Godhead. And here, too, is the entrance to the spirit world, the way to transformation.

Ancient Jewish esoteric cosmology holds that the rock of Jerusalem, where the Temple of Solomon was built, was a place of utmost sanctity. In Talmudic tradition, this great stone, this "Pot-lid of Hell" as it was called, sealed the entrance to the underworld. Christian legend, recounted in one of the lost books of the Bible, states that Christ went down into the Underworld at this site to free the righteous who were imprisoned below, the so-called "Harrowing of Hell." According to the Book of Nicodemus, Christ entered the Underworld through the gates of iron over a rock shaft at the center of the world and worked his way downward to Hell through a complex series of passages very like a labyrinth. Some scholars claim that this Judeo-Christian symbolism was borrowed from the Greeks and is associated with the myth of Theseus and the Minotaur, but it may also be related to Mithraism, a pre-Christian Roman cult associated with the sun, whose members switched over to Christianity when it came to Rome. Mithras, who has the same birth date as Christ, incidentally, went down into the underworld and slew a demonic bull and returned safely to the upper world, bearing a boon for humanity. But in fact the symbolism may go back even farther, to the Neolithic period, or even back to the Paleolithic and the deep, bear-haunted caves that were so much a part of Paleolithic spiritual life.

In all of these cases, though, the imagery is the same. There is a winding pattern of passages, either above the earth or below it, and these turn ever inward to some center, and there is something living there, often some horned creature, and the hero, no matter what the tradition, has to encounter this demon and sometimes fight it and overcome it. Then, either through battle or through a more peaceable meeting, the hero gains knowledge or power, retraces his steps, and returns to the world carrying with him good fortune for all humanity.

At Lykaion in the Greek Isles there was an oracle that was presided over by a nymph named Erato, a prophetess who could explain to the traveler the divine mysteries. This oracle was informed by a goatlike Arcadian deity who lived in the wild hills beyond the protected zone of the village boundary and who invented musical pipes. He was, of course, none other than that old demon trickster, Pan, the devil-horned god who rages through the forests of the world on windy nights and sends panic through the herds and hapless, lost wanderers. Pan was one of the traditional horned guardians of the Omphalos, and if you were able to get to this center and come face to face with him, as did any number of heroes, including Ratty and Mole, you could cross a threshold and step into the sacred zone of the spirit world and gain the source of knowledge of the universe.

Whether you remember this event or whether you get out again after the encounter depends on the clew.

The Italian Renaissance garden designers always left one section of the grounds, the so-called *bosco*, in a natural state, complete with native trees and a dense undergrowth of wild shrubs and herbaceous plants. In England this idea of a taste of the wilderness, a recreation (literally), was introduced onto the estates by the designs of Capability Brown, which were then carried to the Americas and worked into some of the New World gardens, as in the tiny grounds of the eighteenth-century Paca Garden in Annapolis, Maryland.

On those English estates where the older gardens endured, some of the seventeenth- and eighteenth-century hedge mazes survived, most specifically the great labyrinth at Hampton Court. Traditionally in England and other northern countries, in the smaller, turf mazes or rock mazes, the designers would place a symbolic structure in the center, at the goal. In some of these it was simply an old millstone, symbolic, perhaps, of the ancient idea of the Pot-lid of Hell, the entrance to the cave or underworld.

During the evolution of the various gardens on Scratch Flat, I found such a stone, a huge old thing with a square hole in the middle, probably used as a grinding stone by one of the farmers who lived on this land in times past. I found the stone near the foundation of a caved-in barn that was on the property when I first moved there. Over one summer with the help of a Herculean friend of mine, I took down the remains of this barn and used the wood to build various other structures—a chicken house, and later a trellis across the back of the house to grow wisteria. As the central post foundation stone, I used the old grinding stone.

Times changed, things fell apart, I moved out of the house, and my ex-wife, overwhelmed by too many plants and too many projects of her own, tore down the trellis, leaving the old stone sadly unused. But I had an idea for it. I freed it from the ground, propped it up on edge, and slowly, foot by foot, like an Egyptian slave, rolled it up the hill to my garden. My ex bid it farewell with gratitude.

Once in the garden I proceeded to roll the stone the whole length of the maze, turn by turn, course by course, slowly progressing toward the center. It was worrisome work; had it capsized at any point in its journey it would have crashed down upon one of my precious Siberian elms and left the maze with a great gaping hole, which, no doubt, visiting maze walkers would have used as a shortcut. But as it was it did not fall, and eventually I reached the goal. I poised the millstone there on edge for a few seconds and then let it flop down in the center.

In its first winter there I placed a bird feeder on it and walked out every day to fill it. This created an interesting visual attraction, a great swirl of birds funneling around the center of the maze before spiraling down into the goal, out of sight for a while, only to rise up again in a gyre of blue and gray. But, as one mystic friend of mine commented, it seemed sad to weave your way through all of those twists and turns and come face to face with a mere stone. So I decided that what I really needed in this site was a statement of the wilderness, the wildness of this place. I needed an emblem of escape, of danger perhaps, of passion and mystery and energy, music and ecstatic dance and ancient rhymes and rhythms. I needed an image of contact with the old forces that rule nature. What I needed was a statue of Pan.

That began a long search of antique garden statuary centers, and of catalogs and rumors. There was a fine Pan, syrinx, evil smile, and all, under the pines of the nearby Fruitlands Museum in Harvard, Massachusetts. One outlaw friend of mine offered to help me steal it some night. No one paid much attention to it, he pointed out, and it had languished there for decades, winter, summer, spring, and fall, unblessed by staff and unnoticed by visitors. It would take people months to realize that it was even missing. This same friend had suggested some years earlier that I steal the old capitals from the pillars at the Codman estate Italian garden, which I had also coveted. Moral turpitude notwithstanding, in both cases I had mentioned to the staff of these institutions, some of whom knew me, that if ever they had no use for either the capitals or the statue of Pan, I would be happy either to buy them or to store them in my own garden until such time as they had use for them. This meant that if ever they went missing, I should be the prime suspect, although finding Pan in my garden would take a bit of work. First you'd have to find the maze, then you would have to thread your way through it, and then, there in the goal, still grinning, and probably happy in his new home, you would find the missing Lord of the Wood. Although I liked very much the image of a uniformed police contingent weaving its way though my maze courses, guns drawn, in search of Pan, I allowed him to remain in his pine grove, where he belonged.

Long after Scratch Flat is developed and this is the last wilderness in town, perhaps he will come of his own accord.

There is a Christian legend that deals with Pan. In some versions it takes place at the birth of Christ, in others it occurs on the day of the Crucifixion and the renting of the temple veil, but in any of these various forms it involves travelers, usually sailors. In one story, pilgrims are voyaging off the coast of Tuscany. In another they are approaching the Oracle at Delphi. And in another, one of the earliest, they are near the coast of southern Italy, becalmed off the island of Oaxi.

As the sailors approach the coast, the wind suddenly drops, the air thickens, the vessel is becalmed, and an odd stillness hangs over the land and sea. All day the sailors wait, and then toward evening a great thundering voice rings out in the upper air and rolls across the nearby hills and vales declaiming the news:

"The Great God Pan is Dead."

Suddenly, from all the hills and streams, from the little hidden valleys, from temples and sacred groves, from mountain pastures and ferny cliffs and brakes, from bubbling brooks and spring banks, from every wild quarter of Italy there rises a great singular, tragic cry of lament, a vast outpouring of wailing and weeping and shrieking that echoes across the hills and valleys and spreads all across the Italian peninsula. Pan, Pan is dead.

After this event the Greek oracles no longer prophesy accurately. The old gods of the peninsula, the genies of all the old sacred places, the Dianas of the Wood, the nymphs of all wild nooks, the dryads and hamadryads of the trees, the oreads of caves and grottoes, the naiads of the lakes and streams, the fauns and satyrs and centaurs, and all the wild things, fall silent and retreat. The Lord of the Wood is dead, the ancient god of the wild, and the world now has in his place a new king whose domain is not earth but heaven.

There has been much analysis of this alleged event and the story has been altered by folklore and legend so that the locale has changed and also to some extent the period in which the event took place. But as is often the case with myth, the folklore is a reflection of history. The old order was indeed dying, and the new, heaven-inspired, mystic religion of the followers of Christ was near at hand.

John Milton sums up this moment in his poem "Hymn on the Morning of Christ's Nativity" with a description of the shepherds in their pastures, thinking on mighty Pan, followed by the forlorn silence of the oracles after Christ's birth. Milton describes the hollow prophecies of Delphos, the lonely, god-deserted mountains, the sound of weeping and lamenting from all the haunted springs and dales. All the storied spirits of these sacred spots retreat with a sigh. Flower-tressed nymphs with flowing hair mourn in the tangled thickets, and the ancient, powerful gods of the pre-Hellenic tradition—Astarte and Tamuz, Isis, Horus, and Anubis—begin lamenting with a drear and dying sound. Wild nature and its minions and all its gods, demigods, nymphs, satyrs, and centaurs retreat, sorrowing, in the face of the coming of the true God.

"Pan, Pan is dead, the Great God Pan is dead" is a phrase that was picked up and used later by poets and playwrights. And it is probably true that the classical world of which Pan was so much a part, the old images that appear again and again in the niches and rooms of Italian gardens, and in fact the whole metaphor of the Italian gardens themselves with all their underpinning of mythology and history may be lost. As you wander around the museums, public parks, and gardens of Europe you spy the graven images of all of these forgotten gods and heroes, old Pan and Procreus, Artemis and Titan and Neptune, and half the tourists you encounter, probably more, don't know who is chasing who and who got turned into a tree by whom having been chased by which god. I include myself in this group, even though I grew up with these stories—my mother having instilled them in me ever since I was able to understand.

But throughout it all Pan was never really lost. The ancient Lord of the Wood is everywhere in the modern world, even if he has to take the image of the devil himself. And anyway, the real Pan, the spirit of Pan, the spirit of the wild, has never been so alive. Thoreau knew all about him and his fellow gods and demigods. He didn't dare venture any farther up Katahdin because of the overbearing presence of the Olympian Gods. Emerson found him in Italy and brought him home to America, so did Hawthorne, so did Cole, and Church and Muir. Rachel Carson knew about Pan, so did Edward Abbey and old Paul Brooks and all the other twentieth-century advocates of wilderness and wild nature. The soul of Pan, his energetic, fecund spirit, was effectively reborn in the as yet unspoiled open reaches of nineteenth-century America, those wilderness temples of John Muir and company.

Pan is very much with us. And it is not necessary to outfit expeditions into the remnant wilderness at the uttermost ends of the earth in order to find him. Just go out to some nearby dark wood on a moonless night, bushwhack thirty yards into the thickets without a flashlight, stand still for a few minutes, and wait.

He'll be there.

Et in Arcadia ego.

About the Author

JOHN HANSON MITCHELL, author of *Ceremonial Time*, has written four books dealing with the natural and human history of a single square mile of land in eastern Massachusetts known as Scratch Flat. He is editor of *Sanctuary* magazine, published by the Massachusetts Audubon Society, and the winner of the 1994 John Burroughs essay award. In 2000 he won the New England Book Award for the body of his work.